Understanding the
End Times

Bob Yandian

BOB YANDIAN
MINISTRIES

Understanding the End Times

Bob Yandian
Bob Yandian Ministries
9610 S Garnett
Broken Arrow, OK 74012

ISBN:
Printed in the United States of America
Copyright © 1991 by Bob Yandian

Bob Yandian Ministries
9610 S Garnett
Broken Arrow, OK 74012

Table of Contents

1

The Seven Dispensations

One of the most incredible doctrines in the Word of God is the rapture of the church. The Bible teaches that we are to exhort, comfort, and encourage one another by teaching on the fact that Jesus is coming back for the church.

However, as exciting as end time events are to study, the rapture is not a heaven or hell issue. You do not have to believe in the rapture of the church to be born-again, but are encouraged in the Word of God to study end time events.

I Would Not Have You Ignorant

Three verses in the New Testament begin with the phrase, "I would not have you ignorant". The first is found in 1 Corinthians, chapter ten, verse one. *"Moreover, brethren, I would not that ye should be ignorant, how that all our fathers were under the cloud, and all passed through the sea."*

This verse is a reference to the time when Moses led the children of Israel through the Red Sea. As the Red Sea parted, they were actually under a cloud of water and surrounded on each side by water. The entire chapter is on types and shadows, and this particular example is an Old Testament type of New Testament baptism.

The second time this phrase is found is in chapter twelve of First Corinthians. Verse one says, *"Now concerning spiritual gifts, brethren, I would not have you ignorant."* The chapter continues by explaining the spiritual gifts.

The third time this phrase is used is in 1 Thessalonians, chapter four, and verse thirteen. This verse deals with the rapture of the church. *"But I would not have you ignorant, brethren, concerning them which are asleep, that ye sorrow not, even as others which have no hope."*

In each case, the phrase, *"I would not have you ignorant"* actually means, "I know you're ignorant about this topic, but you don't have to be." Paul is simply saying, "These three topics are not difficult to understand, but men make them difficult." What three topics are more misunderstood and divisive than Old Testament types and shadows, the gifts of the Spirit, and end time events?

To understand end time events, you must understand God is a God of order. God is a God of logic. To understand end times, we need to begin with the subject of dispensations. God has divided events into time periods.

The Seven Dispensations

Hebrews 1:1-2:

God, who at sundry times and in divers manners spake in time past unto the fathers by the prophets,

Hath in these last days spoken unto us by his Son, whom he hath appointed heir of all things, through whom also he made the worlds.

There is some controversy over who wrote the book of Hebrews, but I believe Paul was the author. In writing Hebrews, Paul was addressing a group of people who understood the Old Testament, but they did not understand much about the New Testament. The Hebrew believers had difficulty transitioning into the new covenant and were constantly trying to mix the old and new covenants together. Both Paul and Peter had problems dealing with the Hebrew Christians because even though these believers had accepted Jesus as their Lord and Savior, it was difficult for them to break away from the law of Moses. They did not understand that the time period of the law had already been fulfilled.

Hebrews 1:1:

God, Who at sundry times and in divers manners spake in time past unto the fathers by the prophets.

The Greek word for the phrase, *"Who at sundry times..."* is *polumeros*. The Greek word for the phrase, *"...divers manners"* is *polutropos*. Both words begin with *polu*, which means "simple or varied". This verse could be translated, *"God, Who in different time periods and in different ways, spoke in time past, unto the Jewish fathers, through the prophets."*

Hebrews 1:2:

Hath in these last days spoken unto us by the Son, whom he hath appointed heir of all things, by whom also he made the world.

In verse one we have the Old Testament and in verse two we have the New Testament. Verse one calls the Old Testament *"time past"* and verse two calls the New Testament, the day we live in, *"these last days"*. On the Day of Pentecost, the church age was also referred to as the *"last days"*. In Acts 2:16-17, Peter said, *"But this is that which was spoken by the prophet Joel; And it shall come to pass in the **last days**, saith God, I will pour out of my Spirit upon all flesh: and your sons and your daughters* *shall prophesy, and your young men shall see visions, and your old men shall dream dreams."*

Verse one of Hebrews tells us that the Old Testament was divided into many time periods, but the New Testament covers only one time period.

The Old Testament: *God, Who in different time periods, and in different ways spoke in time past..."* (Hebrews 1:1)

The New Testament: *"Hath in these last days spoken..."* (Hebrews 1:2)

These two verses speak volumes. First, the Old Testament was divided into different time periods and within each time period, God spoke differently. In other words, God spoke in different ways in different time periods. The Old Testament is primarily directed toward the Jews and the New Testament toward the Gentiles. Verse one also tells us God spoke through the prophets in the Old Testament. In the New Testament God has mainly spoken to us through the Lord Jesus Christ.

There are varied viewpoints on a number of subjects in the Bible among Christians based upon their denominational background, but one thing every Christian agrees on is the coming of the Lord Jesus Christ. Scholars from both the classical Pentecostal and non-Pentecostal viewpoints are also in agreement that God has divided time into seven dispensations or time periods.

The first dispensation is called the *dispensation of innocence*. This is the time period in which God created man and placed him on the earth. Genesis, chapter one through Genesis, chapter three covers this dispensation. The *age of innocence* ended at the fall of man.

The second dispensation is the *dispensation of conscience*. This dispensation began at the fall and ended at the flood. During this time period, every man did what right according to his own eyes; every man did what he thought was right in his own heart.

Human government is the third dispensation. This time period occurred after the flood. Men began to repopulate the earth, set up their own form of government, and built the Tower of Babel. This dispensation ended when God confused the language of men and scattered them throughout the earth.

The next dispensation is the *dispensation of promise*. During this time period, God isolated a man named Abraham. Through Abraham God began two races in the earth. God spoke to Abraham and said, "Look up at the sky and try to count the stars." Abraham responded, "God, I can't count the stars!" God spoke again and said, "Look at the ground...count the grains of sand on the beach. So shall your seed be. Your seed will be as the stars of heaven and as the sands of the sea." The stars of heaven represent a spiritual race and the sands of the sea represent a natural race. From one man, Abraham, came two innumerable groups of people, the Jewish race and believers.

The Jewish race was the last physical race that began on this earth, but it did not begin naturally; it began supernaturally! Every other race resulted when God scattered mankind at the Tower of Babel, but He set apart one man and changed him from a Gentile into a Jew! How did God do this? What suddenly made Abraham a Jew? The Jewish race came into existence by faith and is the *only* race whose origin was by faith. By faith Abram's named was changed to Abraham.

The word "Hebrew" means "one who crossed the river." God simply said, "Get out of your home country and go to a land that I will show you." Abraham was only partially obedient. When God said, "Leave your kindred, leave all of your family behind you, and go to a land I will show you," Abraham brought his "kindred" with him. He brought his father and he brought his nephew, Lot. Abraham camped in Haran until his father died and *then* went into the promised land, but he still took Lot along with him, which resulted in strife between their herdsmen and also between Lot and Abraham.

One would assume since Abraham was a Jew and a man of faith, all of his children would also be Jews, but that was not the case. One son was a Jew and the other was a Gentile. Isaac was not a Jew because he was born to Sarah. Neither was Ishmael a Gentile because he was born to Hagar, who was a bondmaid. God does not look at physical birth; He looks at faith. Isaac trusted the Lord, Ishmael did not. Isaac was a believer; Ishmael was not.

The Word of God proves this point. In the next generation, Jacob was a Jew, Esau a Gentile. Both came from the one wife. Jacob had twelve sons through two wives and two handmaids, and all twelve were Jews. All twelve were believers. God does not look at your physical birth or your natural background; He looks at your heart.

Your great lineage, background, or position in life does not merit eternal life. Neither does a poor background or position in life. Being born on the wrong side of the tracks, being raised without a father or mother, being raised in a foster home, or having financial lack do not cause you to be rejected from the kingdom of God. The Bible is filled with nobodies who God made somebodies by simple faith.

Again, God isolated a man named Abraham and gave him a promise that through his seed God would raise up a spiritual *and* natural race. This all happened during the *dispensation of promise*, which ended when the children of Israel went into Egyptian bondage.

The fifth dispensation is the *dispensation of the law*. In this dispensation, God gave Moses the law. Galatians 3:19 says the law was added *"till the seed should come to whom the promise was made."* It is important to understand the law was given only until the Seed, Jesus Christ, should come. The *dispensation of the law* ended at the cross.

When Jesus said on the cross, *"It is finished,"* He was not referring to the plan of salvation. The plan of salvation was not complete until Jesus sat down at the right hand of the Father. When Jesus said, *"It is finished,"* He was referring to the Old Testament Law. At that point, Jesus had fulfilled every law and every sacrifice. When He said, *"It is finished"* the law was over. Then the veil was torn from the top to the bottom, the Holy Spirit came, and a new dispensation began.

The sixth dispensation is the dispensation in which we are living; it is the *dispensation of the church.* This time period is also referred to as the *dispensation of grace.* This particular dispensation has existed for some two thousand years and will end at the rapture of the church. After the church age ends, the earth will go into seven years of tribulation.

Then the final dispensation will begin and last for a thousand years. It is the Millennium. This will end the revolt of Satan. At the end of the Millennium, Satan will be released for a season and will fight one last time against the Lord Jesus Christ, but he will be defeated.

The Common Thread Between the Dispensations

There is one common element between every dispensation: God starts it and man ends it. In every dispensation, God successfully begins the dispensation and man successfully brings it to an end. In other words, each dispensation begins with righteousness and ends with sin. *Innocence*

1

God created man perfect. Man sinned. God began the dispensation of conscience, man sinned and God had to bring judgement, which ended with the flood. Then came human government, but man decided that he would build a tower up to heaven to be like God, so God had to confuse the language and scatter men across the earth. During the dispensation of promise, God began anew with one man named Abraham. But through disobedience and sin, the children of Israel went into Egyptian captivity for 400 years. Next, God gave the law, which lasted until God proved that man could not keep it. So, Jesus came and went to the cross to fulfill the law for us! We now live in the church age, but as soon as this dispensation ends, the rapture of the church will occur and for seven years the earth will go into a time of the Tribulation. When the Tribulation ends, we will enter into the final dispensation, which will be the Millennium and it will last for a thousand years. Satan will revolt one last time at the end of the Millennium and from that time, there will be no more dispensations.

A New Heaven and a New Earth

Revelation, chapters 20 and 21 describe the new heaven and new earth. God is going to destroy the earth we currently live on and He will destroy it by fire. The new earth that will emerge will have no more oceans or seas, no more water covering the surface. There will be no sun to light the earth by day and no moon to light it by night. In fact, there will no longer be daytime and nighttime. Heaven itself will come and rest over the earth forever and forever! Earth will be lighted by God's glory.

James 1:17 tells us that God is *"the Father of lights, with whom is no variableness, neither shadow of turning."* In the new earth there will be no shadows! How is it possible to be in a place where there are no shadows? Can you imagine walking down the streets of gold and not seeing your shadow? Can you imagine seeing trees with no shadows? The glory of God will provide light from every direction; you will be completely surrounded by light! The glory of God will shine upon the whole earth; darkness will not be found anywhere. The glory of God will literally cover the entire planet!

Hebrews 1:10-12:

And, Thou, O Lord, in the beginning has laid the foundations of the earth; and the heavens are the works of your hands

*They shall perish; but you remain; and they all shall
wax old as doth a garment;*

*And as a vesture you will fold them up, and they shall
be changed: but you are the same, and your years
shall not fail."*

In these verses, the earth is being compared to clothing.
What happens when you buy a new shirt or a new dress?
You buy it, you wear it, it gets dirty, and you wash it. You
wear it again, it gets dirty, and you wash it. You do this
over and over again until the garment finally wears out
and you get rid of it. Think about this: If clothes never got
dirty, they would never wear out!

In the same way, God created the earth, man got it
"dirty," and God washed it. In the next dispensation, God
cleaned up the earth, gave it to man, man got it dirty,
and God washed it again. After seven times of washing,
God will finally say, "If I wash this thing any more, it is
going to fall apart!" God will take it, fold it up, and get
rid of it. He will give us a new planet that will never wear
out because there will be no more Satan, demons, sin, or
nature of the flesh. We will no longer have a natural body;
we will have our resurrection bodies. The earth will be
perfect and Heaven itself will rest over the earth; Heaven
cannot rest over an imperfect planet.

The Different Ways God has Spoken

Again, Hebrews 1:1-2 says, *"God, Who in different time periods and in different ways spoke in time past unto the fathers by the prophets, has in these last days spoken to us by his Son, whom he has appointed heir of all things, through whom also he made the worlds."*

Not only has God spoken in different time periods; He has spoken in different ways to man. During the dispensation of innocence, God walked with man daily in the Garden during the cool of the day (Genesis 3:8). Adam and Eve sinned and were expelled from the Garden and the *dispensation of conscience* began. God no longer walked and talked with man every day, but He did speak to man from heaven. He spoke to Noah directly from heaven, but man would not repent from his sin and the dispensations of human government and the promise began. During this time, God spoke through types and shadows.

The Angel of the Lord, (Jesus Christ), would often manifest in the earth and speak to man. It was the Angel of the Lord who spoke with Abraham concerning the cities of Sodom and Gomorrah. Abraham was not speaking to an angel. He was speaking to the Lord Jesus Christ, a pre-incarnate visitation of Jesus.

During the dispensation of the law, God would speak out of the cloud, through lightning and thunder. He would speak through the rock that followed the children of Israel (1 Corinthians 10:4). He spoke in many different ways.

By the time we come to the church age, which is the day we are living in, the main way God speaks to us is by the Word. The second way He speaks to us is by the indwelling Holy Spirit living in us. Our spirit bears witness with the Holy Spirit that we are the children of God. God can also speak to us through visions, dreams, and the gifts of the Spirit, but the primary way He speaks to us is through our inward spirit and the Word of God.

During the Millennium, Jesus Christ will personally return to earth and sit on the throne, ruling and reigning in Jerusalem for a thousand years. We will be in the presence of the Lord Jesus Christ during this time.

It is important to understand one important fact: *the way God approaches man is different in every dispensation, but the way man approaches God has never changed; it is always by faith.*

Once again, Hebrews 1:2 says, *"Hath in these last days spoken unto us by his Son, whom he hath appointed heir of all things, by whom* (through Jesus Christ) *also he made the worlds."* The word *"worlds"* is the Greek word *"aion"* and should be translated "ages." We get the English word "eons" from this word. "Eons" means "ages.".This verse is telling us that not only did Jesus Christ create the earth, the animals, the fish, the birds, the universe, and man, Jesus Christ created time.

14

"Through whom also God, through Jesus Christ, created the ages." In other words, every dispensation was created by the Lord Jesus Christ because all things were made by Him and for Him. *All things.* Visible. Invisible. Thrones. Dominions. Principalities. *All things were made by Him and for Him, and without Him was not anything made that was made* (John 1:3).

Hebrews, chapter 11, expounds on the heroes of faith. Again, the way in which God has approached man has been different in every dispensation, but we learn something from Hebrews, which spans the various dispensations.

Hebrews 11:1-2 says, *"Now faith is the substance of things hoped for, the evidence of things not seen. For by it* (faith) *the elders obtained a good report."* The elders are the heroes of faith. The elders are Noah, Abraham, Isaac, Rahab, David. The different heroes of faith appearing in this chapter are referred to as *"elders,"* and by faith, each one obtained a good report. The phrase *"good report"* simply means they obtained a good testimony. This entire chapter is filled with their testimonies.

By faith Abraham sojourned. By faith Noah built an ark. By faith Sarah trusted in God and it was accounted to her for seed, that she bore a child. By faith Rahab received the spies with peace. The elders each spanned a different dispensation. We know that faith comes by hearing and hearing by the Word of God, but none of these heroes had the printed Word. For some, hearing came through signs and wonders. For others, it came though God speaking out of a cloud. Every time God approached man, it was to build faith in his heart so man could approach God by faith. Those saved in the Old Testament were saved in the same way believers are saved in the New Testament: *by faith.* Abraham was saved by faith. Noah was saved by faith. David was saved by faith.

Hebrews 11:3 says, *"Through faith we understand that the worlds were framed by the word of God, so that things which are seen were not made of things which do appear."*

Most often, when people read this verse they translate it as God having created the planets. But the Greek word for *"worlds"* is "aion."

The Greek word for *"word"* is *"rhema,"* which is the *spoken* Word of God. In other words, *"By faith we understand that the ages were framed by the spoken Word of God."* What is this verse saying? By faith God made all the time periods and framed them in. He knew ahead of time when each time period would begin and when it would end. He framed them by the spoken Word of God. God knows in His heart when the church age will end. God knows because it has all been planned and then framed by the Word of God. The greatest relief to our heart should be in God knowing the future, even if we do not. He knew when the church age began and He knows when it will end. God has the whole plan in order and has framed it with His spoken Word!

2

The Dispensation of the Mystery

The Church Age

I want to isolate one particular period of time called the "church age," which is also referred to as the *dispensation of the mystery*. The church age began on the day of Pentecost and will end at the rapture of the church. This dispensation has lasted for approximately two thousand years, and I personally believe it is very rapidly coming to an end.

The *dispensation of the mystery* is the sixth dispensation and is also referred to as the *dispensation of grace*. Just as all other dispensations, the *dispensation of grace* is framed by the spoken Word of God.

Everything was made by the spoken Word of God. God the Father did not create anything; Jesus Christ created everything.

Colossians 1:16-18:

> *For by him were all things created, that are in heaven, and that are in earth, visible and invisible, whether they be thrones, or dominions, or*

principalities, or powers: all things were created by him, and for him:

And he is before all things, and by him all things consist.

And he is the head of the body, the church: who is the beginning, the first-born from the dead; that in all things he might have the preeminence.

Jesus created everything, and He created everything for Himself. God the Father spoke it; Jesus Christ actually made it come to pass. He even created time. Jesus Christ created the church age and since all things were made by Him and for Him, He also created the church! Jesus said, *"I will build my church; and the gates of hell will not prevail against it"* (Matthew 16:18). The church age is unique; there has never been a dispensation like it.

Ephesians 3:1-2:

For this cause I Paul, the prisoner of Jesus Christ on behalf of you Gentiles,

If you have heard of the dispensation of the grace of God which is given me to you-ward.

The word *"dispensation"* means "a time period." It is the Greek word *"oikonomia."* The first part of that word, *"oiko"* means "house." The second part, *"nomia,"* means "law" or "the one who sits in law over the house." A better translation of this word would be "administrator."

Every four years, when the administration of the White House changes, the White House itself does not change, the leadership, along with the administration, changes. Just as the physical building does not change when the new administration comes in, neither does the earth. With each dispensation, the earth remains the same, but an entirely new administration enters and the way in which God deals with man changes.

On the Day of Pentecost when the Holy Spirit was sent to dwell in man, a new administration began. The way God approaches man in our dispensation is strictly by grace. God has approached man by law. He has approached man through human government, but today God approaches man by grace. This does not mean God was not a God of grace in the Old Testament and it does not mean God does not have laws today. The primary way He is dealing with us is by grace. This also does not mean God does not deal through governments today, however again, the primary way He is dealing with the earth today is through the church and through the dispensation of grace.

During the dispensation of the law, God displayed grace. David and Bathsheba, under the law, should have

21

been stoned to death. Not only did David commit adultery, he committed murder; there were two reasons for stoning him according to the law. Instead, David found favor in God's eyes through the confession of his sins. Because of his repentance, he found grace in the eyes of the Lord. Man looks at the outward appearance, but God looks at the heart.

Ephesians 3:3-4:

How that by revelation he made known unto me the mystery; (as I wrote before in few words,

Whereby, when you read, you may understand my knowledge in the mystery of Christ).

The word "mystery" is found sprinkled throughout the New Testament. The word, "mystery" is a transliteration of the Greek word, "musterion." This word has been confusing for many Christians. Most people would define "mystery" as something we don't understand or know. However, in the New Testament the word means "something that was hidden in other dispensations, but has been revealed in this dispensation."

The Pearl of Great Price

In Matthew 13:11, Jesus introduced seven different parables and taught church age truths in some of those parables. There are two parables following one another; one parable makes reference to Israel and the other makes reference to the church.

In one parable, Jesus told the story about a certain man who sold everything he had to buy a treasure, which he hid in a field by burying it. The treasure in this parable represents Israel.

In the next parable, there was a certain merchant who sold everything in order to purchase one pearl of great price. The pearl represents the church. A treasure comes from the land. Diamonds, rubies, sapphires, emeralds, each of the different jewels in the breastplate representing the twelve tribes of Israel, are all found buried in the earth.

A pearl is found in the sea. What is the difference between different gems and a pearl? Gems are formed but a pearl is built. A pearl begins with one little irritating stone; His name is Jesus. He went to hell for three days and three nights and completely irritated the devil. Since that time, the church has been built upon Him one layer at a time. He is the central focal point of the church. Once the pearl is finally formed, the only way to remove the pearl is to lift it out of its place. One day, Jesus will return

23

and lift that finished pearl, the church, and at that time, the church will be complete.

While the pearl has been being built, the treasure has been hidden. However one day, Jesus will dig up the treasure one last time and deal with it for seven years. That period of time is called the Tribulation. This will be the last seven years of Jewish history.

The Parable of the Vineyard

Even though Israel has been buried and Jewish time suspended, God has not done away with them. Prior to the Day of Pentecost, Israel was God's central focus. Jesus came to His own, but His own received Him not. In Matthew 21, Jesus told the parable of a man who owned a great vineyard. The owner turned the vineyard over to the husbandmen while he was gone to a far country. One day he sent servants to receive the fruits of the harvest. The husbandmen killed all three servants, so the owner sent more servants with the same outcome. Finally, he sent his son, thinking the husbandmen would respect his son. Instead, they also killed his son, believing they would get the entire inheritance.

As Jesus shared this story, He asked the Pharisees, "What do you think the owner of the vineyard should do?" They responded, "He ought to take the vineyard away from those wicked men and give it to someone who

24

cares." Jesus said, "That is exactly what will happen. God will take His kingdom from you and give it to a nation that cares." The kingdom of God was taken from the Jews and given to us, the Church. The Church comes from every kindred, tribe, tongue, and nation. The Church came from the seas of all mankind, and the pearl has been being built for two thousand years. But again, after the pearl is completed and lifted out, Jewish time will be reinstated for seven more years.

Paul's Great Responsibility

Ephesians 3:3-6:

> *How that by revelation he made known unto me the mystery; (as I wrote afore in few words,*

> *Whereby, when ye read, ye may understand my knowledge in the mystery of Christ)*

> *Which in other ages was not made known unto the sons of men, as it is now revealed unto the holy apostles and prophets by the Spirit;*

> *That the Gentiles should be fellow-heirs, and of the same body, and partakers of his promise in Christ by the gospel."*

25

Colossians 1:25:

Whereof I am made a minister, according to the dispensation of God which is given to me for you, to fulfil the word of God.

"Whereof" refers back to the previous verse, speaking about the church. In other words, it was for the sake of the church that *"I am made a minister, according to the dispensation of God..."* Again, the word "dispensation" is mentioned.

The verse continues, *"...which is given to me for you, to fulfill the word of God."* The word "fulfill" is the Greek word "pleroma" and it means, "to fill a deficiency."

The best way to illustrate this is to picture an empty glass. Think of this empty glass as the Word of God. Moses came and filled it up with Genesis, Exodus, Leviticus, Numbers, and Deuteronomy. Then Joshua came along and added more. Next, David came and added the Psalms and Proverbs. Then came the major and minor prophets. Some time after that came the Matthew, Mark, Luke, and John who added the gospels.

Paul was given much responsibility in his life. In 2 Corinthians 11:23-28, Paul mentioned all of the pressures and trials he suffered. In verse 28 Paul says, *"Beside those things that are without* (being beaten, shipwrecked in prison, etc.), *that which comes upon me daily, the care of all the churches."* I believe the greatest pressure on Paul's life was completing the Word of God. Imagine the pressure of standing with Moses, David, Isaiah, Jeremiah, all the prophets of the Old Testament, Matthew, Mark, Luke, and John. Imagine the pressure of God tapping you on the shoulder and saying, "Paul, I would like you to complete the Bible; I would like you to fill the deficiency." By the time Paul began writing the epistles, the glass was two-thirds full.

Colossians 1:25-27:

> *Whereof I am made a minister, according to the dispensation of God which is given to me for you, to fulfill* (complete) *the word of God;*

> *Even the mystery which hath been hid from ages and from generations, but now is made manifest to his saints:*

> *To whom God would make known what is the riches of the glory of his mystery among the Gentiles; which is Christ in you, the hope of glory.*

Paul is saying, there is a dispensation unknown in the Old Testament. David did not know it was coming. Moses did not know it was coming. The angels did not know it was coming. Even the twelve disciples did not know it was coming, although Jesus alluded to it several times. It was a surprise to Satan; he also did not know it was coming. Only God the Father, Jesus Christ, and the Holy Spirit knew about the coming of this dispensation.

When the dispensation of grace began, the "rules" changed. Since the "rules" changed, we have a section of the Bible written specifically for our dispensation. Acts, chapter two through Revelation, chapter three, are the books covering the "mystery". The epistles are the "meat" for our dispensation. Chapters one, two, and three of Revelation address the seven churches, but by the time we get to chapter four, the churches are no longer mentioned. The next description is of heaven, where the Church has been taken. At this point, the earth returns to Jewish time.

History of the Greek Word "Musterion"

The Greek word "musterion" (mystery), is one of the oldest Greek words found. The word goes back to Homeric Greek. The origin of "musterion" goes back to ancient fraternities. These ancient fraternities had teachings only accessible to members. When a man joined a fraternity, he was sworn to secrecy concerning anything that went on in the secret meetings.

Fraternities have existed for many, many years even back to the time of Solomon's Temple. When Daniel was taken captive in Babylon, he was made a member of a fraternity known as astrologers. This fraternity studied science; they studied the stars, they studied mathematics. Because Daniel was so brilliant, he was inducted into this fraternity. This fraternity lasted for thousands of years and we find their descendants, the magi, the wise men, mentioned in the book of Matthew.

Why did King Herod and all Jerusalem notice the wise men? First, it was unusual for the wise men to leave the east. Secondly, the Bible never tells us there were only three men as we have been traditionally taught. The wise men typically traveled in caravans of fifty to one hundred men. When these men arrived in Jerusalem they said to Herod, "We are looking for Him that is born King of the Jews." If these men would have said, "We are looking for the King of the Jews," rather than, "We are looking for Him that *is born* King of the Jews," Herod would have responded, "I'm the one you are looking for." But Herod was not born a king; he usurped the throne. In fact, Herod was not a Jew.

These men were so far from the area of their normal travels, it took them two years to reach Jerusalem. They followed a star in the east. Since they studied the stars, one day when a new star appeared, they knew this meant that the Messiah had been born. They followed the star to Jerusalem and finally, found their Messiah in Bethlehem.

Herod wanted the wise men to tell him where they had found the Messiah, but instead, they left Bethlehem by a different way than they had come. The reason Herod ordered all the male children two and under to be killed was because Jesus was two years old! I hate to destroy the image of both the wise men and shepherds at the manger, but the wise men were not there; they did not arrive in Bethlehem until Jesus was already two. Matthew 2:11 says, *"And when they were come into the **house**, they saw the **young child** with Mary his mother..."*

The gold, frankincense, and myrrh the fifty or more wise men brought with them is what sustained Jesus and His family for the next two years in Egypt , where God had led them.

The Greek word for *"wise men"* is *"magi."* This is where we get the English word, "magic." The magi were part of an ancient fraternity who were brilliant men in the study of mathematics, science, and true astrology. By "true astrology" I mean, the true study of the stars to learn of God and the plan of redemption. It was never God's intention for us to look to the stars for direction each day; that is why He sent the Holy Spirit.

Modern astrology is Satan's perversion of God's original intention. Each sign of the Zodiac actually paints the plan of redemption. Virgo the virgin, speaks of the

30

virgin birth of the Lord Jesus Christ. Aquarius holding the water pot, represents the Holy Spirit being poured out on the Day of Pentecost. Sagitarius has a bow and arrow. If you follow the path of the arrow, it is aimed at the heart of Scorpio, who represents Satan. Directly above the head of Scorpio is a heel.

In Genesis 3:15 God says, *"And I will put enmity between thee and the woman, and between thy seed and her seed;* **it shall bruise thy head, and thou shalt bruise his heel."** The heel is about to crush Scorpio's head, which represents the entire plan of salvation. God intended the stars to paint the gospel.

Unfortunately, because the magi belonged to a fraternity, the secrets of what they taught were lost when they died.

Included in the Mystery

If you could draw an imaginary circle around the church, everything contained within that circle is part of the mystery. Again, the mystery begins on the Day of Pentecost and ends at the rapture of the church. A number of areas are included as part of the mystery of the church.

The Indwelling of the Holy Spirit: Jesus gave a prophecy to His disciples. He told them, "I must go away so that I can send the Holy Spirit to you and when He comes, He will be *with* you forever and He will be *in* you"

(John 16:7). Notice, present tense: "He is *with* you." Future tense: "He will be *in* you." Throughout the Old Testament, the Holy Spirit had always been with believers, but it was not until the Day of Pentecost that the Holy Spirit could live *in* men.

The Individual Priesthood of Every Believer: In the Old Testament there was a priestly tribe, but God was looking forward to the time when every believer would be a priest. Peter tells us, *"You are a chosen generation, a royal priesthood, a holy nation, a unique people, that you should show forth the praises of God"* (I Peter 2:9). This is part of the mystery. Things unknown in the Old Testament are revealed in the New.

The Infilling of the Holy Spirit: In the Old Testament there was never the infilling of the Holy Spirit with believers speaking in tongues. Isaiah prophesied of it, but never experienced it. The Holy Spirit was *with* the Old Testament saints, but He was not *in* them.

Spiritual Gifts for Every Believer: In the Old Testament, only the prophet, the priest, and the king could operate in the gifts of the Holy Spirit, but with the new covenant, every believer can operate in the gifts of the Spirit.

The Church: The church, which is also called the body of Christ, did not exist in the Old Testament. It began on the Day of Pentecost and is being added to every day as people receive Jesus Christ as their Lord and Savior.

The New Birth: The new birth did not exist in the Old Testament. Second Corinthians 5:17 says *"...if any man be in Christ, he is a new creature: old things are passed away; all things are become new."* The new birth is part of the mystery.

Not Included in the Mystery

The Death of Jesus Christ: The death of Jesus is not included in the mystery because it was prophesied in the Old Testament (Psalm 33, Isaiah 53) and occurred prior to the Day of Pentecost.

The Resurrection of Jesus Christ: The resurrection is not part of the mystery because it too, is documented in the Old Testament and occurred before the Day of Pentecost.

Jesus Seated at the Right Hand of the Father: Psalm 110:1 says, *"The Lord said to my Lord, Sit at my right hand, until I make thine enemies thy footstool."* Basically God was saying to Jesus, "Sit down for two thousand years until the devil is put completely under Your feet." Even though David prophesied it by the Spirit of God, he did not understand what that event meant. This is not part of the mystery because it was spoken of in the Old Testament and it also occurred just before the Day of Pentecost.

The Tribulation: This event takes place after the rapture of the Church and is well documented in the Old

Testament. Most of the chapters, verses, and descriptions of the Tribulation are found in Zechariah, Joel, Isaiah, and Ezekiel; great and lengthy chapters describing the Tribulation.

The Battle of Armageddon: The greatest battle ever fought in the history of mankind is the Battle of Armageddon. It is not part of the mystery because it takes place at the end of the Tribulation.

The Second Coming of Jesus Christ: The time period in which Jesus comes to earth to establish His kingdom, occurs at the end of the Tribulation and is not part of the mystery.

The Millennial Reign of Jesus Christ: There will be a thousand years of peace where Jesus rules and reigns on earth, called the Millennium. Some of the greatest passages on the Millennium are found in Isaiah, Ezekiel, and Zechariah.

If an event occurs before the Day of Pentecost, it is not part of the mystery; if it occurs after the rapture, it is not part of the mystery.

First Corinthians 15 is an entire chapter on the resurrection, the rapture of the church.

1 Corinthians 15:51-53:

Behold, I shew you a mystery; We shall not all sleep, but we shall all be changed,

34

In a moment, in the twinkling of an eye, at the last trump: for the trumpet shall sound, and the dead shall be raised incorruptible, and we shall be changed.

For this corruptible must put on incorruption, and this mortal must put on immortality.

These verses describe the rapture of the Church and refer to it as a "mystery." It will be the final event before the mystery ends. Again, the mystery begins with the outpouring of the Holy Spirit and ends with the rapture of the Church.

The Old Testament prophets spoke of the Second Coming of Jesus but none of them talked about the rapture because it was hidden. Even Jesus did not discuss the rapture; He talked about His Second Coming. If Jesus *had* talked about the Rapture with His disciples, they would not have understood because they did not understand what the church was, much less the rapture of the church.

I believe we are drawing very near to the end of the dispensation of the mystery—to the end of the Church age. Very soon, the earth will return to the remaining seven years of the Jewish age followed by the Second Coming, and that thousand year millennial reign of the Lord Jesus Christ.

3

The Rapture of the Church

The Old Testament does not teach about the rapture of the church but it does teach on the Second Coming of the Lord Jesus Christ. The reason the Rapture was not taught in the Old Testament is because it is part of the mystery. Neither is the Rapture taught in the Gospels. We may find some types and shadows of it, but there are no specific teachings. To learn about the rapture of the church, we must study the New Testament epistles.

Confusion About the Rapture

There are actually two comings of the Lord Jesus Christ yet to occur. The church is looking forward to the Rapture, which is part of the mystery and the end of the dispensation of grace, also known as the church age.

Again, 1 Corinthians 15:51 says, *"Behold, I show you a mystery. We shall not all sleep, but we shall all be changed in a moment, in a twinkling of an eye."*

There is going to be a time period in the earth called the Tribulation. Seven years from the start of the Tribulation the Second Coming of the Lord Jesus Christ will occur.

The books of 1 and 2 Thessalonians were written to the church in Thessalonica. The believers at Thessalonica were confused about the rapture of the Church, just as many believers are today. False teaching abounded and many were presenting the Rapture in a way that brought fear to the people. Different theories about the Rapture were taught as fact. There were many people in that day who believed they had missed the Rapture and were living in the Tribulation.

During the time 1 Thessalonians was written, many believed the Rapture was very near because Nero was on the throne and Christians were being persecuted. Believers in that day understood that there would be a revival of the Roman Empire during the Tribulation and believed Nero was the Anitchrist. Many believed the Rapture was so near they quit their jobs and were just waiting for the event to come to pass.

Paul wrote 1 Thessalonians in order to correct false teachings and wrong theories being spread concerning the rapture of the church. Paul thought one letter would be sufficient to correct the wrong thinking of believers, but after he had written the first letter to the Thessalonians, someone wrote a false epistle attributing it to Paul. This false epistle basically said, "Some of the things I taught you in the first epistle were wrong and I have changed my mind. The Rapture has already occurred and we are living in the Tribulation. Nero is the Antichrist and the persecution of the Christians is evidence of the fact that we are living in the Tribulation." Because of this false epistle, people were in fear. Paul wrote 2 Thessalonians to inform believers he had not changed his mind and what he had written in 1 Thessalonians was true.

2 Thessalonians 2:1:

Now we beseech you, brethren, by the coming of our Lord Jesus Christ, and by our gathering together unto him...

Paul said, *"...we beseech you...by the coming of our Lord Jesus Christ, and by our gathering together unto him."* Notice, Paul is specifically referring to the rapture of the Church because there will be no "gathering together" at the Second Coming. The Rapture is so important that he uses it as a rallying point for Christians.

At the rapture of the church, Jesus does not come to earth; He appears in the sky. At the Second Advent, He will literally come, touch the earth, and remain here. At the rapture of the church, Jesus will appear and we will rise to meet Him in the air. What a blessed event that will be! Every day we should wake up with an anticipation that this could be the day Jesus appears. At the same time, we should have a realization that He may not appear today; therefore we need to remain busy as a witness in the earth.

If someone very credible came and said, "Jesus appeared to me today and told me to tell everyone He is coming back on Monday" most of us would probably rush to call all of our friends and relatives to try to get them born again.

The point is, Jesus could come at any moment. He could come today; He could come in the next thirty minutes! The Rapture should be the greatest inspiration for witnessing available to us.

When I attended Trinity Bible College, one of my instructors was Charles Duncombe who had traveled with Smith Wigglesworth. He told us the testimony of a powerful minister he had been familiar with in England. This man had been an agnostic; he did not believe in the things of God. He believed God existed somewhere but had no need for Him. His mother, who was a believer, had witnessed to him for many years. His father and many friends also witnessed to him, but he refused to accept the Lord. When his mother was dying, he went to her bedside and just before she breathed her last breath she said to him, "Don't take the mark of the beast."

After she died he thought, "What in the world is the mark of the beast?" He tried to find it in the Bible but since the Bible was unfamiliar to him, he did not find the answer. He went to a preacher and asked him to explain the mark of the beast to which he responded, "The mark of the beast is in the book of Revelation. A day is coming when Jesus will come and remove the church from the earth and an evil, wicked man will dominate the earth. If you ever take the mark of the beast in your hand or forehead, you can never be saved; you can never be born again and you will go to hell and the lake of fire forever and forever."

Hearing the explanation, the man got so nervous he began sweating, went home, fell on his knees and that night accepted Jesus Christ as his Lord and Savior. He became one of the greatest ministers in England. It was through an understanding of end time events that this man was saved!

2 Thessalonians 2:1:

*Now we beseech you, brethren, **by the coming** of our Lord Jesus Christ, and by our gathering together unto him...*

2 Thessalonians 2:8:

*And then shall the wicked One be revealed, whom the Lord shall consume with the spirit of his mouth, and shall destroy with the brightness **of his coming**.*

Notice, there is a *coming* in verse one and a *coming* in verse eight. At the coming in verse one, the church is gathered to Him, but at the coming in verse eight, Jesus will destroy the Antichrist by the brightness of His coming. In verse one we have the rapture of the church and in verse eight we have the Second Coming. In verses two through seven we have all the events that occur between the two comings.

2 Thessalonians 2:2:

That you be not soon shaken in mind, or be troubled, neither by spirit, nor by word, nor by letter as from us, that the day of Christ is at hand.

Paul is simply saying, "There is a mindset that seems to have spread throughout the church that you are living in the Tribulation. Do not be moved by the different winds of doctrine that are circulating. Also, people are distorting the Word of God to support the theory that the Tribulation has come." Paul continues, "I don't care if there is a letter contradicting my first letter, it is wrong. Don't let anyone shake you up and convince you that the Tribulation has arrived, because it has not. Don't be soon shaken in mind."

Every time any major war arises, people begin to shout, "We're in the Tribulation!" When Hitler rose to power, many said, "He is the Antichrist." When Mussolini rose to power they said, "Mussolini is the Antichrist. He is a ruler from Rome, and Rome is the revived Roman Empire,

therefore he *must* be the Antichrist!
people were saying that the Russian leader,
the Antichrist because he had a birthmark on

In our generation and throughout the centuries
try to take circumstances and make them fit the Wo
God, when instead the Word of God should be the standa
by which circumstances are judged.

Antichrist will be Jewish. Why would the Jews accept
him as their Messiah if he were not a Jew? John said,
"...there are many antichrists" (1 John 2:18). Until *the*
Antichrist is revealed, there will be many false prophets
operating in the demon spirit of Antichrist. Hitler and
Mussolini were antichrists; they were not *the* Antichrist.
Hitler had to have been demon possessed, but when *the*
Antichrist is revealed in the earth, he will be possessed by
Satan himself! Not only will Satan possess this man, he
will operate through him with mighty signs and wonders,
but they will be lying signs and wonders. Antichrist will
do supernatural things and deceive many people.

2 Thessalonians 2:3:

> *Let no man deceive you by any means: for that day*
> *shall not come, except there come a falling away first,*
> *and that man of sin be revealed, the son of perdition.*

n deceive you in any
etter as if from us."
:rse is a reference to

ill return while there
ophecie have come
:s around the world
time of evangelism

and soul winning the world has ever seen, which will
sweep us right into the rapture of the church. However,
many people look at verse three and say, "No, this verse
says Jesus can't come until there is a great falling away
first. Many are going to turn away from Him first and
because of the great apathy in the earth, He is going to
return."

The Departure

The problem people encounter with this verse is the
phrase "falling away." The Greek word for this phrase is
not a verb; it is a noun. The Greek word is "apostasia" from
which we get the English word "apostasy." Throughout
the New Testament, when the Greek word "apostasia" is
used, it has a negative connotation. For instance, Hebrews
3:12 says, *"Take heed, brethren, lest there be in any of
you an evil heart of unbelief, in departing from the
living God."* The word, "departing" is the verb form of

apostasia and is used negatively. However, when the word "apostasia" stands alone, it is neither positive nor negative; its connotation is dependent upon its association with the other words in a sentence.

The word "aspotasia" in 2 Thessalonians 2:3 was translated by the New King James version writers according to all of the other negative uses of the word. In this instance, the word "apostasia" in the noun form does not mean "falling away"; it means "departure."

Putting it back into context, this verse could actually be translated, "Don't be fooled by any means, for the Tribulation cannot come until the departure occur first." The "departure" is speaking of the rapture of the church.

Kenneth Wuest's Expanded Translation of the New Testament brings out the tense, mood, and voice of the original Greek. His translation of this verse says, *"That day cannot come until the aforementioned departure of the church occur first."*

The *"aforementioned departure of the church"* was mentioned in verse one by His coming and *"our gathering together unto Him."*

Verses three and eight combined could be translated, *"...for that day cannot come until the departure occur* **first,** *and that man of sin be revealed, the son of perdition,* **and then**...*that Wicked be revealed."*

Antichrist cannot be revealed until we are gone. Think about that; he cannot even be revealed until the church is gone! No wonder Jesus said, *"I will build My church and the gates of hell shall not prevail against it"* (Matthew 16:18).

Each individual believer is so powerful in the earth that even if only one Christian were left on earth, Satan would be powerless to reveal Antichrist until that one believer was removed. I personally believe the worldwide religion mentioned in Revelation is the New Age Movement we are seeing in our day. I believe this movement will sweep right into the Tribulation and their "messiah" will be the Antichrist, but their messiah cannot be revealed until ours returns for His church.

2 Thessalonians 2:3-4:

Let no man deceive you by any means: for that day shall not come, except there come a falling away first, and that man of sin be revealed, the son of perdition.

Who opposes and exalts himself above all that is called God, or that is worshipped; so that he as God sits in the temple of God, shewing himself that he is God.

Verse four actually occurs in the middle of the Tribulation. After three and a half years, the Antichrist will actually walk into the temple, sit in the place that

Messiah the Christ is supposed to sit, and declare himself to be God. He will force the people to worship him.

2 Thessalonians 2:5:

> *Remember ye not, that, when I was with you, I told you these things?*

Paul is simply saying, "What I told you in I Thessalonians still stands. I haven't changed my mind."

2 Thessalonians 2:6:

> *And now you know what withholdeth that he might be revealed in his time.*

Paul continues by saying, "You know what is withholding him and hindering him from being revealed. It is you, the Church!"

2 Thessalonians 2:7:

> *For the mystery of iniquity is already at work: only he who hinders will continue to hinder until he be taken out of the way.*

Here is that word "mystery" again. Just as there was a transition between Jesus and the church, there is a transition between the church and the Tribulation. We see seeds of Antichrist in the earth today, seeds of rebellion. Those "seeds" are *"the mystery of iniquity already at work."*

He Who Hinders

Who is the "he" who is hindering? Many have said it is the Holy Spirit Who is hindering. That is partially true. The church is hindering and the Holy Spirit *in* the church causes believers to be so powerful, the Anitchrist cannot be revealed.

Some teach the Holy Spirit is the One Who is hindering and He will hinder until He be taken out of the way. The problem with this teaching is the Holy Spirit will never be taken away. It is true the Holy Spirit lives in the church, but His presence is also in the world. When the church is taken to heaven, the Holy Spirit will remain. There will be many saved during the Tribulation. There will be signs, wonders, and miracles during the Tribulation. Two witnesses will come to earth empowered by the Holy Spirit to perform signs, wonders, and miracles. There will never be a time when the Holy Spirit is removed.

The "he" who hinders is the church. Some might immediately ask, "Yes, but isn't the church a *she* and not a *he*?" The answer is no. The church will not become the bride of Christ until *after* the Rapture. Right now we are the body of Christ and Jesus does not have a male head and a female body! All of the teaching about the church being the Bride of Christ is still prophetic. We will be fashioned into the Bride after the rapture of the Church when we go through the judgment seat of Christ. Revelation 19 tells us *then* we will come back as a bride adorned for her husband. Until then, we are the Body of Christ.

In essence, we are Christ in this earth. The Bible says we are ambassadors, standing in His place in the earth. Didn't Jesus say, "The works I do, you will do also, and greater?" The word "Christian" means "little Christ". We are Christ's hands. We are Christ's voice. We are His works. We are His body. Therefore, we are the one hindering. The church is as much a hindrance to the works of Satan in the earth as Jesus was when He was present on earth. They tried to kill Jesus. They tried to push Him over a cliff, but they could not kill Him. He voluntarily died on the cross and until then no one could kill Him.

The Antichrist cannot be revealed until we are removed. Satan can bring persecution against us, but he cannot remove the Church. The more he brings persecution, the more powerful we become. Not only are believers praying for the rapture of the church, Satan is! He is looking forward to the church being removed so he can operate as he desires in the earth.

Although 2 Thessalonians 2:1-8 is a great overall description of the Rapture, 1 Thessalonians 4:13 is one of the most familiar verses on the rapture of the church.

Those Who are Asleep

1 Thessalonians 4:13:

But I would not have you ignorant, brethren, concerning them which are asleep, that you sorrow not, even as others which have no hope.

When you find the word "asleep" in the New Testament, it is a reference to the death of Christians. Sinners are said to be *dead*. Christians may be called "dead in Christ," but usually when reference is being made to a Christian who has died, they are said to be "asleep." This sleep is not a "soul sleep," it is a reference to the body. The reason the term "asleep" is used is because if someone is sleeping, it means they will eventually wake up. Sinners are never said to be asleep because they will not have a wake-up day. They are dead and will be further dead one day. They are spiritually dead and one day they will be eternally separated from God.

Believers are spiritually alive; even death cannot separate us from that life. Again, when the Christian dies

God says he is "asleep." One day he will awaken and the great awakening is the rapture of the church.

Understand this, when a Christian dies and they are placed in the ground, it is normal to have sorrow, but we do not sorrow as those who have no hope. Many have buried mothers, fathers, husbands, wives, and children. Even though sadness comes, it cannot remove the joy residing inside at knowing the separation is only temporary. We will only be separated for a few years and then we will see our loved ones again.

King David said, when his young child died, "I will go to be with him, but he shall not return to me." Even David knew one day he would see his child in heaven. We will see our friends and relatives who have died in Christ in heaven one day.

Today, we frequently refer to a Christian funeral as a celebration; a celebration of *"to live is Christ and to die is gain"* knowing believers will be with Jesus Christ forever and forever. It is also part of God's plan for the Christian family to cry. Even in the Old Testament God told Israel to stop and mourn the death of Moses for forty days. Mourning is normal. Weeping may endure for a night, but joy does come in the morning. We should never judge a Christian who is in mourning and say, "They shouldn't be crying. What a lack of faith!" It is natural to miss the person who is gone. When we cry, it is not for the person who has gone on; it is really for those who are left behind.

1 Thessalonians 4:14-15:

> *For if we believe that Jesus died and rose again, even so them also which sleep in Jesus will God bring with him.*

> *For this we say unto you by the word of the Lord, that we which are alive and remain until the coming of the Lord shall not prevent them which are asleep.*

The word "prevent" means "precede." We will not precede those who are asleep—those who have died. Verse 16 goes on to explain.

1 Thessalonians 4:16-18:

> *For the Lord himself shall descend from heaven with a shout, with the voice of the archangel, with the trump of God: and the dead in Christ shall rise first:*

> *Then we which are alive and remain shall be caught up together with them in the clouds, to meet the Lord in the air: and so shall we ever be with the Lord.*

> *Wherefore comfort one another with these words.*

The Family of God

The body of Christ is still on the earth, but one day we will rise to meet the Lord in the air. Ephesians 3:14-15 says, *"For this cause I bow my knee unto the Father of our Lord Jesus Christ, Of whom the whole family in heaven and earth is named."* As long as we are on the earth, we are part of the body of Christ, but the minute we leave, we are no longer part of the body of Christ. The body does not exist in heaven, but the family exists in *both* places. You may leave the church and you may leave the body of Christ, but *you never leave the family of God.* You will be in the family of God forever and forever! The church is temporary, the body of Christ is temporary, but the family of God is eternal. Again, the family of God is temporarily divided; part of the family is on earth and part is in heaven.

Ephesians 3:14-15:

For this cause I bow my knees unto the Father of our Lord Jesus Christ,

*Of whom the **whole family in heaven and earth** is named.*

Even though the family of God is temporarily separated, there is coming a day when the whole family of God will be together. That day will be the rapture of the church.

1 Thessalonians 4:15:

For this we say unto you by the word of the Lord, that we which are alive and remain until the coming of the Lord shall not prevent them which are asleep.

When Jesus Christ comes at the Rapture, all those dead in Christ will come with Him. Those who are "asleep" will receive their bodies out of the grave and the moment they rise from the grave, we which are alive and remain will be caught up together with them in the air. People have often believed the Rapture was only for those who remain alive on the earth, but it also includes those who have gone on before.

The Shout, The Voice, and the Trump

1 Thessalonians 4:16:

For the Lord himself shall descend from heaven with a shout...

"The Lord himself..." This is such a significant event, Jesus Christ will personally perform it. Prior to this time Jesus delegates the gospel, the church, the five-fold ministry, witnessing, laying hands on the sick; all He has equipped the body of Christ to do He has delegated

to believers. He is now in heaven making intercession for us, but one event coming is so important He will do it Himself.

First Thessalonians 4:16 says again, *"For the Lord himself shall descend from heaven with a shout…"* Notice, this verse does not say, "The Lord will descend from heaven and *then* shout…" It says He will descend from heaven *with a shout.* The Bible says that Jesus does not know the day or hour; only the Father knows. Even the angels do not know when the Second Coming will occur. If Jesus does not know when the Second Advent will occur, He must not know when the Rapture will be. He knows that the Second Coming will take place seven years after the rapture, so He cannot know when the Rapture will occur.

I picture Jesus daily asking the Father, "Is today the day?" When the Father answers "No," Jesus continues making intercession for the saints, performing all of the duties He has in heaven, and bringing our prayers before the Heavenly Father. For some two thousand years I can picture Jesus asking the Father, "Is this the day?" However, the day is coming very soon when the Father will answer, "Today is the day!" When that happens Jesus will descend from heaven shouting through the entire universe until He hits the atmosphere of the earth. The entire church on earth will hear the voice of Jesus Christ as He descends from heaven with that shout!

First Thessalonians 4:16 continues, *"...with the voice of the archangel."* Notice, *"archangel"* is singular. Some may not agree with this thought, but the Bible seems to suggest there is only one archangel and his name is Michael. Some would question, "What about Gabriel?" He is a high angel, a messenger angel. He is certainly important, but the Bible never refers to him as an archangel.

This verse indicates Michael has something to say, but it does not indicate what he will actually say.

Jude 9:

> *Yet Michael the archangel, when contending with the devil he disputed about the body of Moses, durst not bring against him a railing accusation, but said, The Lord rebuke thee.*

The book of Deuteronomy describes the death of Moses. God actually buried Moses. It is not explained until thousands of years later when Jude received a revelation from the Holy Spirit, that something happened in the atmosphere the moment Moses died. Satan wanted the body of Moses. I believe the reason he wanted Moses' body was because he knew the children of Israel would probably make his body an icon and would end up worshipping Moses rather than God. Satan would have loved for the children of Israel to follow after the memory of a man rather than God. Why would Satan have access to a man's body? It is because our bodies still have a curse in them. Because of Adam's rebellion against God, man has had the nature of the flesh. Satan has a right to the body because it holds a curse and he is the one who initiated that curse. We do not lose the nature of the flesh when we are born again. The only way we lose the nature of the flesh is when we die physically or when we receive our resurrection bodies.

When Moses died, the curse had not been lifted from the earth. That is why Satan came and said, "I want his body." God did not even give Satan the time of day. Instead, He said, "Michael, you handle this one." As Michael and Satan contended over the body of Moses, Michael said, "The Lord rebuke you." With that statement, Satan had to shut his mouth and God buried Moses' body in the area of Pisgah. The Bible says no one knows to this day, where Moses was buried, because God buried him!

When the Rapture occurs, it is very possible Satan will contend for our physical bodies. I can imagine Satan saying, "You can have their spirits, but I want their bodies." I can hear Michael once again saying, "The Lord rebuke you!" To ensure that Satan will not have our physical bodies, He is going to fashion our physical bodies into resurrection bodies, which have no curse. Satan will not and cannot have a legal right over our resurrection bodies.

First Thessalonians 4:16 continues, *"...with the trump of God."* God will be blowing a trumpet! People have said, "This has to be Gabriel blowing the trumpet," but this verse unmistakably says God will blow this trumpet.

In the Old Testament, trumpets were used for two purposes. First, they were used for an assembly to gather people together. Second, it they were used to announce war. I believe the trump of God will fulfill both of these purposes. There will be a gathering together of the body of Christ unto the Lord, and then, as soon as we reach heaven, there will be a declaration of war. God cannot declare war until all believers are removed from the earth.

1 Thessalonians 4:18:

Wherefore comfort one another with these words.

It has been very common for ministers to use the rapture of the church to scare people into the kingdom of God, but this verse of scripture tells us that teaching on the Rapture should bring comfort to every heart.

Notice, 1 Thessalonians 4:17 says, *"...then **we** which are alive and remain..."* not *"...then **some** which are alive and remain."* This verse indicates the entire Church will be taken up at the rapture. *Every* believer will rise to meet the Lord in the air. God is not going to leave us on earth to destroy us with the enemy. Because we are His ambassadors, He will not leave us on this earth when war is declared. We will rise to meet Him in the air. In heaven God will deal with the entire family at one time at the judgment seat of Christ.

1 Corinthians 15:51:

Behold, I shew you a mystery; we shall not all sleep, but we shall all be changed.

One thing we all have in common as the family of God, whether in heaven or on earth, is that we will all be changed. We will all receive our resurrection bodies at the same time. Some in the family will go by way of death and some will not see death. I personally believe that we are living in that generation that will not see physical death. I believe we are in that generation that will see the return of Jesus Christ.

Two Examples

There are two men mentioned in the Word of God who were raptured from the earth and they are a type of what will happen at the rapture of the church. One man was a Gentile and the other was a Jew. The Gentile was a man named Enoch. He is mentioned in Genesis 5 and Hebrews, chapter eleven.

Hebrews 11:5:

*By faith Enoch was translated that he should not
see death; and was not found, because God had
translated him: for before his translation he had this
testimony, that he pleased God.*

Enoch did not even begin living for the Lord until
he was approximately sixty-five years old. He had a son
whose name was Methuselah. This verse says Enoch was
"translated." The word "translated" means, "taken from
here to someplace else."

Notice the words *"and was not found."* This indicates
that people were looking for Enoch after he was taken to
heaven, but they never found him.

The second man mentioned in the Bible who was
translated was Elijah (2 Kings 2). This is a familiar story.
Elijah and Elisha had been traveling together for some time.
Elisha asked for a double portion of Elijah's anointing.
This was not an unusual request. In Old Testament times it
was understood the firstborn had a number of rights. First,
he was the priest of the family; he had a great inheritance.
Second, he received a double portion. This was part of his
firstborn right. Elijah had no children so Elisha claimed
him as his spiritual father. Elisha also chose to forsake
his family to follow Elijah. When Elijah threw his mantle
around Elisha, Elijah found him plowing with twelve

yoke of oxen. When this happened Elisha ran from the field to kiss his family good-bye. In essence, Elisha was burning his bridges behind him. He probably never saw his parents again. He left everything for the ministry and Elijah became his spiritual father. In the New Testament Paul referred to Timothy and Titus as his sons in the faith. Elisha acted on the fact that Elijah was his spiritual father and said, "I want a double portion". Elijah's response was, "If you see me when I go, you can have it." Elisha did see Elijah taken to heaven. Others saw the event from a distance.

2 Kings 2:16:

And they said unto him, Behold now, there be with thy servants fifty strong men; let them go, we pray thee, and seek thy master: lest peradventure the spirit of the Lord has taken him up, and cast him upon some mountain, or into some valley. And he said, Ye shall not send.

These are sons of the prophets speaking. They are supposed to be the spiritual ones yet they are saying, "Perhaps the Spirit of the Lord lifted him up in the sky and then dropped him somewhere."

2 Kings 2:17:

And when they urged him till he was ashamed (embarrassed), He said, Send. They sent therefore fifty men; and they sought three days, but found him not.

In each of these cases, when these men were translated, people went searching for them but could not find them. These two stories tell us something about the rapture of the church; people will look for us but they will not find us!

Changed in a Moment

1 Corinthians 15:52:

In a moment, in a twinkling of an eye, at the last trump: for the trumpet shall sound, and the dead shall be raised incorruptible, and we shall be changed.

The Greek word for "moment" is "atomo." The English word "atomic" is a derivative of this word. When the atom was discovered, we named it after this Greek word. It was named *atom* because scientists believed it to be the smallest particle in existence. Later, they discovered that the atom consists of even smaller particles called *protons, neutrons,* and *electrons.* Since the discovery of these smaller components, they have discovered yet smaller particles called *quarks.*

The word "atomo" means "something that has been divided so many times it cannot be further divided." Theoretically this is impossible. It is always possible to half things, but this Greek word indicates that something has been divided so many times it can no longer be divided.

The rapture of the church will occur more quickly than one ten-thousandth of a second. In one split second we will be here, and in the next split second we will be gone! The world will see us one moment, and in the next, they will no longer see us! The world will not hear the shout. They will not hear the voice of the archangel. They will not hear the trump of God. The church will hear these things but the world will not. They will continue to live their lives on earth.

The Voice of the Shepherd

John 10:4:

> *And when he putteth forth his own sheep, he goeth before them, and the sheep follow him: for they know his voice.*

John 10:5:

And a stranger will they not follow, but will flee from him: for they know not the voice of strangers.

One day I was talking with a shepherd who described an event I thought was so astounding. He told me every shepherd has his own sound for his particular sheep. He said, "Even though the Bible says, 'My sheep know My voice,' honestly the voice is not a word. Shepherds don't call their sheep by saying, 'Here sheepy, sheepy!' Shepherds use sounds." He then went on to explain that some shepherds use a click, others use a whistle, and others may use nothing more than a clapping of their hands. Whatever sound the shepherd chooses, the sheep come to know as the "voice" of the shepherd. He explained five or six shepherds may gather around a tree for lunch and all of their flocks will mingle together. Sheep are not branded, so there is no way to distinguish one sheep from another. Picture five or six flocks of sheep gathered together in one place. Shepherds are not concerned about the flocks mingling. When the first shepherd leaves, he may whistle and all of his sheep will lift their heads because they recognize his "voice." The other sheep keep grazing as his sheep work their way out from among the other flocks to follow their shepherd. Then the next shepherd makes his sound and only the sheep from his flock lift their heads and follow him.

What a wonderful description of the rapture of the church! Throughout the whole earth people will be "grazing" and Jesus is going to descend from heaven with a shout. Jesus will say, "Come!" and only His sheep will lift their heads and follow Him into heaven. The rest of the world will not realize what has happened.

The Resurrection Body

1 Corinthians 15:53:

> *For this corruptible must put on incorruption, and this mortal must put on immortality.*

Our natural body will be changed immediately into a resurrection body.

Philippians 3:20:

> *For our conversation is in heaven; from whence also we look for the Saviour, the Lord Jesus Christ:*

The Greek word for "conversation" is "politicos," from which the English word "politics" is derived. The word means "citizenship". This verse is telling believers that our citizenship is in heaven.

Philippians 3:21:

Who shall change our vile body, that it may be fashioned like unto his glorious body, according to the working whereby he is able even to subdue all things unto himself.

"Vile body" is a reference to our physical body. Our natural bodies are still under the curse. The Bible has given us a prototype of the resurrection body; the body of Jesus. To learn how our resurrection bodies will operate, we look at the body of Jesus. Our "vile bodies" will be fashioned just like the glorious resurrection body of Jesus Christ.

Colossians 3:4:

When Christ, who is our life, shall appear, then shall ye also appear with him in glory.

This verse is also a reference to the rapture of the church.

1 John 3:1-3:

Behold, what manner of love the Father has bestowed upon us, that we should be called the sons (or the

66

children) of God: therefore the world knows us not, because it knew him not.

Beloved, now are we the sons of God, and it doth not yet appear what we shall be: but we know that, when he shall appear, we shall be like him; for we shall see him as he is.

And every man that hath this hope in him purifieth himself, even as he is pure.

One day Jesus will appear and we will be just like Him. In our spirits we are the sons of God. One day, we will actually be sons and daughters of God in our bodies. That will be the last part of redemption.

Verse three tells us the rapture of the church brings hope. To remove the teaching of the rapture of the church is to remove the hope we have. A portion of scripture from 1 Corinthians 15 explains if the resurrection of Jesus never occurred and our hope in Jesus was only in this life, we would be *"of all men most miserable."* The new birth is wonderful but heaven will be better. As good as the new birth is, as wonderful as prosperity, divine healing, and the gifts of the Spirit are, Paul is saying, "If we only had these things to look forward to we would be miserable." The most wonderful event we, as Christians, have to look forward to is the Rapture will one day occur and we will be with the Lord in heaven for eternity.

The Holy Spirit we have with us and in us today is just an "earnest" of our inheritance. "Earnest" means it is a down payment. The new birth, the infilling of the Holy Spirit, the gifts of the Spirit, the daily walk of the Spirit, the guidance of the Spirit, all of these wonderful things we have been given are merely a small down payment on what heaven is going to be, and the guarantee that the rest is on the way. The rapture of the church moves us into the greatest part of our eternal life, which is eternity with God forever and forever! God not only planned for the church to be a witness in this earth; He planned on the family of God being with Him forever and forever in heaven.

Do not accept any teaching that purports teaching on the Rapture will cause people to sin. First John 3:3 teaches that every man who has hope in the resurrection actually purifies himself. Believers are pure in their spirits, but this verse says when we learn about the Rapture we will have a greater desire to live a pure life.

Romans 8:22:

We know the whole creation groans and travails in pain together until now.

Romans 8:23:

And not only they, but ourselves also, which have the firstfruits of the Spirit, even we groan within ourselves, waiting for the adoption, that is, the redemption of our body.

The firstfruits of the Spirit is the new birth. The redemption of our body is the final phase of salvation. Salvation is three-fold: *Past tense, present tense,* and *future tense.* It is *spirit, soul,* and eventually *body.* First, we are born again in our spirit. Next, we are daily sanctified in our soul. The last part of our salvation is the redemption of our body.

Romans 8:24:

For we are saved by hope: but hope that is seen is not hope: for what a man seeth, why doth he yet hope for?

Ephesians 2:8 and 9 tells us we are saved by faith. What does this verse mean when it says we are saved by hope? This verse is not referring to the redemption of our spirit; it is referring to the redemption of our body. Salvation in our spirit guarantees one day our physical body will be redeemed.

Romans 8:25:

But if we hope for that we see not, then do we with patience wait for it.

This verse tells us as much as we would like to see the rapture, we are to patiently wait for it to occur. How long must we patiently wait for it? Until it happens.

1 Corinthians 15:35:

But some man will say, How are the dead raise up? And with what body do they come?

Every Christian has probably wondered about the resurrection body. It can disappear and reappear, walk through walls, eat and never gain weight! Our resurrection body will be just like the body Jesus has. It can be on earth, travel through space, and go to heaven. It can breathe or not breathe; Jesus breathed on His disciples. It can eat or not eat; Jesus ate with His disciples after the resurrection. Jesus could appear, disappear, or walk through a wall. That is what our resurrection body will be like.

1 Corinthians 15:36-44:

Thou fool, that which thou sowest is not quickened, except it die:

And that which thou sowest, thou sowest not that body that shall be, but bare grain, it may chance of wheat, or of some other grain:

But God giveth it a body as it hath pleased him, and to every seed his own body.

All flesh is not the same flesh: but there is one kind of flesh of men, another flesh of beasts, another of fishes, and another of birds.

There are also celestial bodies, and bodies terrestrial:
but the glory of the celestial is one, and the glory of the terrestrial is another.

There is one glory of the sun, and another glory of the moon, and another glory of the stars: for one star differeth from another star in glory.

So also is the resurrection of the dead. It is sown in corruption; it is raised in incorruption:

*It is sown in dishonour; it is raised in glory: it is
sown in weakness; it is raised in power:*

*It is sown a natural body; it is raised a spiritual body.
There is a natural body, and there is a spiritual body.*

To understand the concept of sowing seed is to
understand the resurrection body. When seed is planted in
the ground, the part of the seed that dies is the shell. Every
seed has its own shell or body. A seed has both a shell and
a heart. The heart does not die, but it cannot come to life
until the shell dies. The plant that arises from the ground
is produced from the heart of the seed. Until the shell dies,
the heart cannot be released; it is from the heart of the
seed that the new plant comes forth.

To understand the resurrection, understand this: *You
are a seed.* I like to think of it this way, *we do not bury
Christians we plant them.* When a Christian dies, the spirit
does not die; the shell dies. Our bodies are made from
nature, the dust of the ground and this is the reason we refer
to our bodies as "natural." Our new resurrection bodies
will be made out of spirit. The human spirit will actually
become tangible and become a resurrection body! That
is why Paul says that our bodies are "sown in weakness
and harvested in power. Sown a natural body, harvested
a supernatural body—harvested a spiritual body. What a
wonderful day we have to look forward to—*the rapture of
the church!*

4

The Judgment Seat of Christ

Sovereignty and Grace

People have often said, "If you believe in the rapture of the church, you'll go and if you don't you'll stay." However, some things in life we receive *by faith* and other things will occur totally unrelated to our faith. Certain things God will do regardless of whether or not we believe Him. For instance, man did not exist when God created the universe and the earth; God did not have to wait for someone to believe Him before the world came into existence. Some things are simply sovereign acts of God.

The entire chapter of 1 Corinthians 12 is about the sovereignty of God. The gifts we operate in and the offices we stand in are not determined by our faith. If God has called us to be an evangelist, but we are believing to be a pastor, we can believe all we want but it will not change what God has already determined for our life. The office in which each person stands is part of God's sovereignty. The Bible says He has placed us in the body of Christ as it has pleased Him. He never asked us what we would like to be!

The operation of the gifts of the Holy Spirit are also part of the sovereignty of God. The Holy Spirit divides the gifts to every man severally as He wills.

Anything connected with the cross is by grace. There is a difference between the grace of God and the sovereignty of God. Whatever God does in sovereignty, we do not have to believe Him for; He will still do it. However, what God does in grace, we must accept by faith. Grace and faith go hand in hand. Anything Jesus did on the cross we must believe and receive. Salvation does not involve the sovereignty of God; we are saved by grace through faith (Ephesians 2:8). God will not force salvation on us. Grace is available to everyone; sovereignty is not. Salvation must be *received.* Healing must be *received.* Prosperity must be *received.* All of these things are a result of the cross and are given by grace, but we must *receive* them by faith.

Here is the point: *Almost everything included in the end times involves the sovereignty of God.* Whether you believe it or not, it will come to pass. The rapture of the church is not grace. The rapture of the church is sovereignty. It is going to happen. Any believers who are alive on earth at the time of the rapture of the church are all going up to meet Jesus in the air and then to heaven. The only way God can get the entire family in heaven and earth together at one time is the rapture of the church. All Christians, past and present, will be brought before the judgment seat of Christ where we will be judged for our deeds done in the flesh.

Without Spot or Wrinkle

Ephesians 5:21-27:

> *Submitting yourselves one to another in the fear of God.*

> *Wives, submit yourselves unto your own husbands, as unto the Lord.*

> *For the husband is the head of the wife, even as Christ is the head of the church: and he is the saviour of the body.*

> *Therefore as the church is subject unto Christ, so let the wives be to their own husbands in every thing (literally, in every area).*

> *Husbands, love your wives, even as Christ also loved the church, and gave himself for it;*

> *That he might sanctify and cleanse it with the washing of water by the word,*

That he (that is Jesus) might present it (that is the Church) to himself a glorious church, not having spot, or wrinkle, or any such thing; but that it should be holy and without blemish.

Look very closely at verse twenty-seven. It does *not* say He is coming back for a church without spot or wrinkle, as people often quote it. This verse says He will *present us to Himself* a glorious church without spot or wrinkle. We will not be without spot or wrinkle until Jesus presents us to Himself at the judgment seat of Christ. There is no such thing as a perfect church on the earth. We will be going through a sanctification process until the Rapture. If Jesus was coming back for a church without spot or wrinkle, the first thing we would have to do is quit getting people saved because they come to Jesus with all of their spots and wrinkles! Sanctification is a process; it usually takes years to get rid of the spots and wrinkles and they are never completely gone until the Rapture. In addition, we would also have to stop getting people saved so we could work on getting all of the spots and wrinkles out of our lives! Jesus is coming back for the church as it presently exists. It will be filled with spots and wrinkles until He removes them at the judgment seat of Christ.

The Judgment Seat of Christ

Romans 4:10-14:

> *But why do you judge your brother? Or why do you set at nought your brother? For we shall ALL stand before the judgment seat of Christ.*
>
> *For it is written, As I live, says the Lord, every knee shall bow to me, and every tongue shall confess to God.*
>
> *So then every one of us shall give account of himself to God.*
>
> *Let us not therefore judge one another any more: but judge this one thing, that no man put a stumblingblock or an occasion to fall in his brother's way.*

In English "judgment seat" is two words, but in the Greek it is only one word. The word is "bema" and does not mean judgment. "Bema" means "rewards." This word would better be translated in English as "rewards seat of Christ."

The history behind this word is very interesting. In the ancient world, the best games were found in Corinth and were the equivalent of the Olympics in our day. The Corinthian games were known throughout the entire world at that time. As young men would cross the finish line they would be ranked by their places; first, second, and third place just like our gold, silver, and bronze medal winners. After crossing the finish line, the winner would go to the bema and stand before it. The king was seated on the bema. This was a high, elevated seat and as the young man would come to stand before him, the young man's head was almost at the same level as the king's knees. As the winner stood before the king, the king would reach over and place a crown on his head. The crown consisted of olive leaves but it represented much more. It meant the man and his family were tax exempt for the rest of their lives. They were also fed, clothed, and educated at public expense for the rest of their lives. They were given free room and board and had permanent seats to the games for the remainder of their lives. Not bad for olive leaves!

2 Corinthians 5:8-10:

We are confident, I say, and willing rather to be absent from the body, and to be present with the Lord.

Wherefore we labour, that, whether present or absent, we may be accepted of him.

For we must all appear before the judgment seat of Christ; that every one may receive the things done in his body, according to that he hath done, whether it be good or bad.

As good as life is, it cannot be compared to heaven. Both good and bad Christians will be in heaven and stand before the judgment seat of Christ. All of us will go to heaven with good works and not so good works. As we stand before the Lord, we will be judged for both good and bad deeds we have done.

First Corinthians 15:51-52 says, *"...we shall all be changed. In a moment, in the twinkling of an eye."* All will be changed and all will stand. Who are the *"all"* that will be changed? Those changed are both the dead in Christ *and* those who are alive and remain. We will all receive resurrection bodies, go to heaven, and for the seven years God is judging the earth, Jesus will be seated on the judgment seat and we will be there before Him.

1 Corinthians 3:9-10:

For we are labourers together with God: ye are God's husbandry, ye are God's building.

According to the grace of God which is given unto me, as a wise masterbuilder, I have laid the foundation, and another buildeth thereon. But let every man take heed how he buildeth thereupon.

The word "husbandry" simply means "garden." We are God's garden and He is still working on us. When you have a garden, you do not just plant something and forget about it. It takes work to have those prize-winning flowers! You cannot plant flowers and just leave them because weeds will grow around them and bugs will come in. We are God's garden and He is still pruning us, planting fertilizer, killing bugs and pulling weeds from our lives. God is constantly caring for us and this is why we as believers continue growing and becoming stronger.

These verses also say we are God's building. We are compared to a building. If you have led someone to the Lord, you have laid a foundation in that individual's life. The foundation is not you, you simply witnessed to them. When they said, "yes" to Jesus, you did your part in helping lay a foundation in their life. Verse ten says again, *"But let every man take heed how he buildeth thereupon."*

1 Corinthians 3:11:

For other foundation can no man lay than that is laid, which is Jesus Christ.

Every one of the Corinthians Paul was addressing had accepted Jesus under his ministry. This is the reason he said, "I have laid a foundation in your life and that foundation is Jesus Christ."

Gold, Silver, Precious Stones, Wood, Hay, and Stubble

1 Corinthians 3:12-13:

Now if any man build upon this foundation gold, silver, precious stones, wood, hay, stubble;

Every man's work shall be made manifest: for the day shall declare it, because it shall be revealed by fire; and the fire shall try every man's work of what sort it is.

Each person has two areas of life they are building. One is called *gold, silver,* and *precious stones.* The other is called *wood, hay,* and *stubble.* Notice, verse eleven says, "...if *any* man." That is singular. Paul did not call anyone by name but he is addressing each individual. There is no break between "gold, silver, precious stones" and "wood, hay, stubble.".Verse eleven does not say, "If one man builds on his foundation gold, silver, and precious stones and another builds on that foundation wood, hay, and stubble..." Every person has two piles. One is called *wood, hay,* and *stubble.* The other is called *gold, silver,* and *precious stone*s which are built on the foundation called Jesus Christ.

1 Corinthians 3:1-3:

And I, brethren, could not speak unto you as unto spiritual, but as unto carnal, even as unto babes in Christ.

I have fed you with milk, and not with meat: for hitherto ye were not able to bear it, neither yet now are ye able.

For ye are yet carnal: for whereas there is among you envying, and strife, and divisions, are ye not carnal, and walk as men?

To identify how we accumulate gold, silver, and precious stones and wood, hay, and stubble in our lives, imagine a circle. Inside the circle represents being in fellowship with God and outside the circle represents being out of fellowship. In fellowship, you are called "spiritual" (verse 1). Out of fellowship, you are called "carnal" (verses 1-3). "Carnal" is mentioned three times in those three verses. How do we get out of fellowship with God? Sin. How do we get back into fellowship with God? First John 1:9, *"If we confess our sins, he is faithful and just to forgive us of our sins, and to cleanse us from all unrighteousness."*

When you are in fellowship with the Lord, you produce good works, which is called *gold, silver,* and *precious stones.* When you are out of fellowship, carnal and under the control of the flesh, you produce what is called *wood, hay,* and *stubble.*

Two people can come to church and one may be carnal and the other spiritual. The carnal person may give one hundred dollars in the offering and the spiritual person may only give five dollars. In this example, the carnal person will receive wood, hay, and stubble for his giving and the spiritual person will receive gold, silver, and precious stones.

It is important not to confuse sin with wood, hay, and stubble. God will forgive your sin, but the wood, hay, and stubble you accumulated while in sin will be judged. Whether you are fasting, praying, giving or doing any other thing deemed "spiritual," if you do these things while in sin, it is empty works. Sin not only includes outward sin, it includes inward sins such as jealousy, bitterness, envy, and strife. Works done in the flesh do not impress God. Faith impresses God. Being spiritual impresses God.

First Corinthians 3:12 again says, *"Every man's work shall be made manifest: for the day shall declare it, because it shall be revealed by fire; and the fire shall try every man's work of what sort it is."*

Notice, the man is not being judged; his works are. We bypassed judgment when we accepted Jesus, but our works will be judged. This verse tells us that fire is going to try every man's work to determine what kind it is. When the fire descends, the wood, hay, and stubble will be burned up. But when the fire hits the gold, silver, and precious stones, they will not be destroyed. Instead, the fire will purify them. The fire will burn up the wood, hay, and stubble before you receive your rewards. You will be rewarded for what remains: the *gold, silver,* and *precious stones.*

Rewards in Heaven

1 Corinthians 3:14-15:

> *If any man's work abide which he hath built thereupon, he shall receive a reward.*

> *If any man's work shall be burned, he shall suffer loss: but he himself shall be saved; yet so as by fire.*

What are these verses saying? After the fire comes down, each person will be rewarded for anything left—the gold, silver, and precious stones! What if nothing is left after the fire burns everything up? What if a person has no gold, silver, or precious stones? That individual will be in heaven, which will be wonderful in itself, but he will receive no rewards. Receiving rewards does not mean you have to run off to a remote country; it does not mean you have to go out every day and feed the poor. Sometimes when we think of good works we think of these mega-deeds. The Bible says if we give a cup of cold water in His name we will receive a prophet's reward. The size of the deed is not important. What is important is the motive behind the deed. I believe many will receive rewards in heaven and will say, "That deed deserves a reward?" And Jesus will answer, "Of course it does because you did the deed out of your love for Me. You didn't have to be prodded. No one had to motivate you to do it. You simply did it out of a heart of love. No deed went unseen by Me."

1 Corinthians 15:41-44:

There is one glory of the sun, and another glory of the moon, and another glory of the stars: for one star differs from another star in glory.

So also is the resurrection of the dead. It is sown in corruption; it is raised in incorruption:

It is sown in dishonour; it is raised in glory: it is sown in weakness; it is raised in power:

It is sown a natural body; it is raised a spiritual body. There is a natural body, and there is a spiritual body.

The rewards in heaven will be vast and varied. Some are going to shine like the sun in heaven, some like the moon, and the rest like the stars. No two will be the same. Just as the stars vary in brilliance and intensity, so will the rewards. Unfortunately, some Christians will have rewards in heaven that will be difficult to see; many Christians will receive few rewards in heaven.

Revelation 7:9-10:

> *After this I beheld, and, lo, a great multitude, which no man could number, of all nations, and kindred, and people, and tongues, stood before the throne, and before the Lamb, clothed with white robes, and palms in their hands;*
>
> *And cried with a loud voice, saying, Salvation to our God which sitteth upon the throne, and unto the Lamb.*

Standing before the Lord on a sea of glass will be an innummerable company of people from every nation, kindred, and tongue wearing white robes and waving palm leaves. They will serve the Lord night and day and praise Him continually. They are going to be shouting because they are in heaven!

There is also a group around the throne of God called the elders. They not only have white robes, they have kingly robes, crowns, and scepters. They will rule and reign with Jesus Christ. I do not want to just make it to heaven. I believe those who rule and reign with Jesus are those who spent time in prayer, walked by faith, attended church, and witnessed to those around them. They will have an abundant entrance into heaven!

2 Peter 1:10-12:

> *Wherefore the rather, brethren, give diligence to make your calling and election sure: for if ye do these things, ye shall never fall:*
>
> *For so an entrance shall be ministered unto you abundantly into the everlasting kingdom of our Lord and Saviour Jesus Christ:*
>
> *Wherefore I will not be negligent to put you always in remembrance of these things, though ye know them, and be established in the present truth.*

That abundant entrance will occur at the judgment seat of Christ—the rewards seat, for the seven years following the rapture of the church, as we each stand before Him to receive our rewards for the good works we have done.

5

Daniel's Seventy Weeks

The Hub of All Prophecy

Daniel 9:24-27:

> *Seventy weeks are determined upon thy people
> and upon thy holy city, to finish the transgressions,
> to make an end of sins, to make reconciliation for
> iniquity, to bring in everlasting righteousness, to seal
> up the vision and prophecy, and to anoint the most
> Holy.*

> *Know therefore and understand, that from the going
> forth of the commandment to restore and to build
> Jerusalem until Messiah the Prince, shall be seven
> weeks, and threescore and two weeks: and the street
> shall be built again, and the walls, even in troublous
> times.*

> *And after threescore and two weeks shall Messiah
> be cut off, but not for himself: and the people of the
> prince that shall come shall destroy the city and
> the sanctuary; and the end thereof shall be with a*

flood, and unto the end of the war desolations are determined.

And he shall confirm the covenant with many for one week: and in the midst of the week he shall cause the sacrifice and the oblation to cease, and for the overspreading of abominations he shall make it desolate, even until the consummation, and that determined shall be poured out upon the desolate.

Most who study end time events consider this portion of scripture to be the hub of all prophecy. There is much information on the end times concentrated into these four verses.

Seventy weeks are determined upon thy people... (verse 24)

The Hebrew word for "weeks" is "shabuwa." Although "weeks" is a good translation, in the context of this verse it does not have this meaning. The word "shabuwa" actually means, "segments of seven." Daniel 9:24 literally says, "Seventy segments of seven are determined upon thy people."

The Hebrew word for "determined" is "chathak," which means, "to cut out." In essence, this verse says, "Seventy weeks are cut out of time."

Daniel 9:1-2:

> *In the first year of Darius the son of Ahasuerus, of the seed of the Medes, which was made long over the realm of the Chaldeans;*

> *In the first year of his reign I Daniel understood by books the number of the years, whereof the word of the Lord came to Jeremiah the prophet, that he would accomplish seventy years in the desolations of Jerusalem.*

Here Daniel refers to "years." There are seven days in one week. One day in Daniel's prophecy is equivalent to one year. Daniel does not completely understand the meaning of the prophecy, but he does understand the number of the "years." We too, can understand.

Babylonian Captivity

At the beginning of the book of Daniel, four young men were taken captive in Babylon: *Daniel, Shadrach, Meshach, Abednego.* Actually, the names "Shadrach, Meshach, and Abednego" were not their Hebrew names; these were the names given to them in Babylon. Daniel was also given the name of Belteshazzar, but he would not use it. He continued to go by his Hebrew name "Daniel."

ese young men loved the Lord and they stood
; of God. Of all who were taken into captivity,
these four men rose in prominence and Daniel rose
even higher than the three other men. It seemed Daniel
continually rose to positions of leadership.

The Babylonians had conquered Jerusalem, and as
was common with most conquering nations, they took
the youngest, brightest, and strongest into captivity and
attempted to teach them to think like the people of Babylon.
The thinking behind this was, "If we can take your best
and most brilliant and change their thinking, you should
just surrender. Look at the power we possess!"

To their shock, the Babylonians could not turn Daniel,
Shadrach, Meshach, and Abednego; they would not bow.
The Babylonians destroyed Jerusalem. They stole the gold,
silver, dishes, goblet--things used for sanctified worship
to God. They burned the temple, killed and massacred
many people. Those who survived were forced to march
to Babylon. Multitudes died on the death march, but
those who survived went into slavery. Captivity lasted for
seventy years and it was during this time God raised up
Daniel to be one of the chief prophets.

Warnings to Israel

Prior to captivity, Isaiah and Jeremiah had both given
prophecies concerning Israel. Isaiah's prophecies were

more positive. He would say, "Turn to the Lord. He will bless you. He will heal you. He wants to do so many wonderful things for you, but you must first repent."

Jeremiah wrote on the negative side. He would go into intricate detail describing fornication that occurred in the groves, giant idols that were set up in the mountains around Israel where the people would come and have mass orgies during the day, women that would become so hysterical that they would burn their own children, the screams of the children mixed with the screams from the sexual activity. The children of Israel had entered into idolatry, worshipping Baal, worshipping the gods of the heathen. Many think of idolatry as burning a little incense before an idol, but almost all idolatry involves sexual perversion. This is what was taking place when Jeremiah addressed the children of Israel. Jeremiah wrote about the perversions and finally said, "This is it...the longsuffering of God has come to an end and you are going into captivity because of your refusal to turn from your sins in repentance."

Jeremiah even prophesied naked for a while. He removed his clothes and buried them, then went back, dug up his clothes, and put them on again. In the prophecy, the clothes represented Israel and Jeremiah represented God. God was in essence saying, "You are so close to Me. You are like My clothing, but I'm going to take you off and bury you. Then I'm going to dig you back up and put you on again." This spoke of the Babylonian captivity. The taking

93

off of the clothes and burying them was Babylon. Digging them up and putting them on again represented Israel being released from captivity. Israel went into captivity for seventy years. After their captivity they never again worshipped idols.

Even though Daniel was taken into captivity as a young boy and grew up in Babylon, he never stopped serving the Lord. Under Nebuchadnezzar, the first king in power during his captivity, Daniel rose to a high position of authority.

During the beginning of his reign, King Nebuchadnezzar verbally made reference to the Lord but did not accept Him as Lord. Each time things were going well, he would become proud, take the glory, and expected everyone to praise him. He reached a point where a curse came upon him. He roamed through the forest and his hair and fingernails grew; he lived like a wild animal for seven years. At the end of the seven years, he came to himself, accepted the Lord, and said "God is the true God." He then returned to the throne.

Writing on the Wall

Following the reign of Nebbuchadnezzar, his grandson, Belshazzar took the throne (Daniel 5). He became very wicked and wanted nothing to do with Daniel. One night Belshazzar was having a wild party. He became bored because this party was the same as all the others and decided to do something different. He said, "Let's get those golden vessels we took from the house of Israel when we destroyed the temple, and let's drink from them." When man begins to use the things of God for sin, it is not pleasing to God.

Suddenly, the party became very quiet. As those present looked toward the wall, they saw a giant hand and it was writing in a language no one understood. The Bible says Belshazzar was so frightened his knees were literally knocking together! As Belshazzar was watching he said, "What is this? What does it mean? Someone interpret it for me." He called for his magicians, astrologers, and soothsayers, but none of them could interpret. They said, "We have never seen this language; we have no idea the meaning."

The queen finally said, "Call Daniel and he will interpret this saying for you." So, Daniel was brought in and he warned, "I will give you the interpretation, but you will not like it." Belshazzar was not deterred by the warning and still wanted to know the meaning. Daniel proclaimed, "Tonight you are weighed in the balances and found wanting. This very night the kingdom will be taken from you and given to another." Belshazzar laughed at the saying. The wall around Babylon was so high and so thick no one had been able to penetrate it. In addition, no one had conquered the Babylonians in years. What Belshazzar did not consider was the river that ran through the city. It ran under the wall, through the city, and back out the other side of the wall. The Medes and Persians damned up the river leaving the riverbed under the wall for them to easily enter. At the very moment Daniel was interpreting the message on the wall, the streets were filled with Medes and Persians who had come into the city under the wall. In one night, the kingdom was taken from Belshazzar and Darius came to the throne under Cyrus the Great. History tells us Cyrus the Great was a believer in the Lord. He was greatly open to the Jewish people. He came into power just prior to the end of the seventy years of captivity from which the children of Israel were about to be released.

Daniel's Vision

During captivity, Daniel had been studying the scrolls of Jeremiah. Jeremiah received a prophecy saying the children of Israel would be in captivity for seventy years. As Daniel studied this prophecy, he realized the seventy years were almost complete. Daniel began to pray and ask the Lord to show him what would happen after they were released. He wanted to know where they were to go and what they were to do to rebuild their lives. God answered his prayer, but He answered it way beyond the time for which Daniel was seeking answers. God gave him a vision that encompassed the time from their release from captivity until the second advent of the Lord Jesus Christ. Daniel received exceedingly abundantly above all he could ask or think!

Daniel could not comprehend the magnitude of what the Lord was showing him. God told him, *"Seventy weeks are determined upon thy people..."* If one day equals one year, seven weeks equals forty-nine years. Therefore, seventy weeks is equal to 490 years. God told Daniel, "Once you are released from captivity, 490 years will pass before the second advent of the Lord."

Immediately, you may say, "Yes, but 490 years have already come and gone and Jesus still hasn't returned!" But what these verses reveal is that the 490 years are divided into segments. It must be emphasized the 490 years would occur *after* captivity. The reason this is significant is because there were 490 years from the death of David until the Babylonian captivity. David represented the pinnacle of the kings of the Old Testament and at his death Israel was at its greatest time ever. Under Solomon's reign, Israel became richer, but they also became more carnal. David was not as wealthy as Solomon, but he was more spiritual. David walked with God and was a man after God's own heart. From the time of David's death, Israel began to degenerate. Degeneration does not begin with big sins; it begins with small sins. God says, "Whatsoever is not of faith is sin." Man may refer to sins as small, but these small deviations eventually lead to greater sin. Although there were some good kings after David's death, generally the nation continued on a downhill slide.

The Results of Compromise

What was the minor deviation that occurred after the death of David? The people had become so prosperous they decided not to allow the land to rest every seven years as God had commanded. They thought they would increase their prosperity by planting their crops every year. They said to themselves, "We know God said to let the land rest every seventh year, but what a waste to just let the land sit there for a year.

We know God said He would make up to us what we do not receive on the sabbatical year, but that land could still be producing and bring us even more prosperity!"

When we compromise in one area, it eventually spreads into other areas. The children of Israel began deviating by not allowing the land to rest every seven years and years later ended up involved in some of the worst idolatry found in the Word of God.

The children of Israel did not allow the land to rest for 490 years, which meant they owed God seventy Sabbaths. Because of their disobedience, they were taken into captivity for seventy years and the land, which they had not allowed to rest, rested. For the seventy years of Babylonian captivity, the land did not produce. Nomads came in, scavengers came in, squatters came in and planted, but nothing would grow. It was not until Israel returned to the land that it began to produce once again. Once they returned, the land became greatly productive, producing the finest fruits and vegetables. The land was simply waiting for the return of God's people.

Seventy Sabbaths

2 Chronicles 36:17-21:

> *Therefore he brought upon them the king of the Chaldees, who slew their young men with the sword in the house of their sanctuary, and had no compassion upon young man or maiden, old man, or him that stooped for age: he gave them all into his hand.*

> *And all the vessels of the house of God, great and small, and the treasures of the house of the Lord, and the treasures of the king, and of his princes; all these he brought to Babylon.*

> *And they burnt the house of God, and brake down the wall of Jerusalem, and burnt all the palaces thereof with fire, and destroyed all the goodly vessels thereof.*

And them that had escaped from the sword carried
he away to Babylon; where they were servants to him
and his sons until the reign of the kingdom of Persia:

To fulfill the word of the Lord by the mouth of
Jeremiah, until the land had enjoyed her sabbaths:
for as long as she lay desolate she kept Sabbath, to
fulfil three-score and ten years.

Again, the reason the children of Israel went into captivity for seventy years is because they owed the Lord and the land seventy Sabbaths.

From the time of David until Babylonian captivity was 490 years. While in captivity God revealed to Daniel, "There were 490 years before captivity and there will be 490 years after captivity. The difference is the 490 years before captivity ended in destruction, but the 490 years following captivity will end in righteousness. The first 490 years ended in captivity but following the second 490 years will be the greatest freedom man has ever seen!"

Following captivity, Israel enjoyed the best years they had ever seen. They were at their zenith right up until the time Jesus Christ came into the earth. Israel's "golden years" lasted over 400 years and were a time of the greatest prosperity Israel had ever experienced. Gold and silver were plentiful and the opening fourteen verses of Deuteronomy 28 were fulfilled in Israel. They were blessed in the city, they were blessed in the field, they were blessed coming in, and blessed going out. They were above only and not beneath and they were able to lend to many nations and not borrow. Although they never returned to idolatry as a nation, they did make Judaism into a legalistic religion bringing bondage, rather than a relationship with God designed to bring great freedom.

When we want to understand prophecy, we must look to the Jewish people. The hub of prophecy is not Rome or the United States; it is Israel. Daniel 9:24 says, again, *"Seventy weeks are determined upon thy people and upon thy holy city..."* *"Thy people"* are the Jews and *"thy holy city"* is Jerusalem. To determine where we are chronologically in reference to the rapture and end time events, we must look to Israel and specifically to Jerusalem and the Jewish people.

Interpretation of Daniel's 70 Weeks

Daniel 9:24:

> *Seventy weeks are determined upon thy people and upon thy holy city, to finish the transgressions, to make an end of sins, to make reconciliation for iniquity, to bring in everlasting righteousness, to seal up the vision and prophecy, and to anoint the most Holy.*

101

Although it has been translated *"...to anoint the most Holy,"* the Hebrew actually says, "...to cleanse the Holy of Holies." This is referring to the final cleansing of the temple, which will occur when Jesus Christ comes to sit on the throne during His millennial reign. God is revealing to Daniel, "Once you are released from captivity, there will be 490 years until the millennial reign of Jesus Christ."

Again, most will automatically begin thinking, "Well, that can't be...490 years have already come and gone."

Daniel 9:25:

Know therefore and understand, that from the going forth of the commandment to restore and to build Jerusalem until Messiah the Prince, shall be seven weeks, and threescore and two weeks: and the street shall be built again, and the walls, even in troublous times.

If Daniel could "know and understand," so can we. God is telling Daniel, "Daniel, the next 490 years will begin when the king gives a decree to rebuild Jerusalem and the sanctuary." The decree was given by King Artaxerxes, in Nehemiah, chapter two. He was a Persian king, who allowed the children of Israel to rebuild the city.

Notice, verse 25 says from the rebuilding of Jerusalem and the sanctuary until the Messiah would be *"seven weeks, and threescore and two weeks."* Threescore and two weeks is equivalent to sixty-two weeks. We have two time periods mentioned in this verse, seven weeks and sixty-two weeks.

Again, the word "week" in the Hebrew is "shabuwa," which literally means "segments of seven." Therefore, if one day is equivalent to one year in Daniel's prophecy and if every week is a segment of seven, then one week equals seven years. If one week equals seven years, seven weeks multiplied by seven is forty-nine years. Verse 25 is saying, "From the time the decree is given until the city is rebuilt will be forty-nine years."

Daniel 9:26:

> *And after threescore and two weeks shall Messiah be cut off, but not for himself: and the people of the prince that shall come shall destroy the city and the sanctuary; and the end thereof shall be with a flood, and unto the end of the war desolations are determined.*

The next time period mentioned in verses 25 and 26 is *"threescore and two weeks."* Again, this equals sixty-two weeks and when multiplied by seven, it is 434 years. It took forty-nine years to rebuild the city and from that time until the Messiah was cut off at the cross was an additional

434 years. Forty-nine plus 434 equals 483 years. Jesus went to the cross at the end of Daniel's sixty-ninth week or 483 years after the decree was given to rebuild the city and then He was cut off.

So, "...*after threescore and two weeks* (sixty-two weeks), *shall the Messiah* (Jesus) *be cut off, but not for Himself.*" If Jesus was cut off, but not for Himself, for whom was He cut off? He took our infirmities and bore our sicknesses. He took our iniquities and sins; He had none of His own. He was not cut off for Himself; He was cut off for us.

Jesus went to the cross at the end of Daniel's sixty-ninth week. He went to the cross exactly 483 years after the decree was given to rebuild the city. He went to the cross and was cut off from God's presence to redeem mankind from sin.

Jesus went to the cross at the end of Daniel's sixty-ninth week. There is one more week of Jewish time remaining. One more seven-year period is yet to be fulfilled. The Tribulation is one and the same as Daniel's seventieth week! Daniel's seventy weeks have not been fulfilled. There are seven years remaining until the fulfillment of his prophecy. Unknown to Daniel, the Old Testament saints and even the disciples, was the church. The church was a mystery and it was inserted between Daniel's sixty-ninth and seventieth weeks.

Isaiah prophesied, *"For unto us a child is born, unto us a son is given: and the government shall be upon his shoulders...Of the increase of his government and peace there shall be no end"* (Isaiah 9:6-7).

Isaiah saw no break between Jesus' birth, life and eternal kingdom. Because both Daniel and Isaiah were unaware of the church age, they saw no break in the seventy weeks or 490 years. Just before Jesus' death on the cross the crowds were yelling, "Hosanna! Hosanna! Hosanna! Blessed is He that comes in the name of the Lord!" They thought Jesus was going to usher in His everlasting kingdom. They were disappointed and upset when He died. They did not understand why His kingdom did not come and did not understand the church age would be inserted, separating Daniel's sixty-ninth week from the seventieth.

Picture God holding two stopwatches. One represents Jewish time and the other the church age. When the decree went forth to rebuild Jerusalem and the temple, God pulled out the Jewish age stopwatch and it began ticking. It ticked and ticked and ticked for forty-nine years. The city was rebuilt, the wall completed, the temple also rebuilt. It continued ticking for another 434 years. At the end of 483 years (Daniel's sixty-ninth week), Jesus went to the cross, said "It is finished" and God stopped the Jewish stopwatch seven years before it was complete.

105

On the Day of Pentecost, God picked up and started the second stopwatch, the church age. The Holy Spirit descended, God started the watch and it has been ticking for some two thousand years! This stopwatch is about to tick its last. Jesus is about to come back for His church. When He returns at the rapture of the church, God is going to stop the watch and throw it away because He will no longer need it. He will then pick up the Jewish stopwatch and restart it and the last seven years of Jewish time will begin to tick away. This is Daniel's seventieth week.

Daniel 9:26:

> *And after threescore and two weeks shall Messiah be cut off, but not for himself: and the people of the prince that shall come shall destroy the city and the sanctuary; and the end thereof shall be with a flood, and unto the end of the war desolations are determined.*

The word "prince" in this verse has a lower case "p" and is a reference to the Antichrist. Notice is says, "... *the people of the prince that shall come.*" Not only is the "prince" mentioned, the "people of the prince" are also mentioned. At the time Daniel wrote this prophecy, Rome was unknown. Daniel could not name Rome but he could describe the people who would come and bring destruction to the city and the sanctuary. The *"prince that shall come"* is the Antichrist who will rule the revived Roman Empire. The Romans controlled the area from Italy, into Europe, Great Britain and as far as Germany. This verse is saying that when the Messiah is "cut off" at the cross, the *"people of the prince that is yet to come"* (Rome) would destroy the temple and the city of Jerusalem.

The church began to rise from the time of the cross and will continue until the rapture, which will occur approximately 2000 years after the cross. Jesus is coming very soon!

Daniel 9:27:

And he shall confirm the covenant with many for one week: and in the midst of the week he shall cause the sacrifice and the oblation to cease, and for the overspreading of abominations he shall make it desolate, even until the consummation, and that determined shall be poured out upon the desolate.

The "many" in this verse is a reference to the Jews. The "one week" here is the seven years of the Tribulation. As the church age comes to a close, Israel will rise again.

During the Tribulation, the earth will revert for seven more years to Jewish time. The temple will exist and sacrifices will again be made because Jewish time

107

will have been reinstated. No longer will God be dealing with the church; He will unearth the treasure, Israel, and operate through that nation once again.

The first converts following the rapture of the church will be twelve thousand out of each of the twelve tribes of Israel. They will immediately receive Jesus Christ as Lord and Savior. Evangelism will go forth from Jerusalem and spread throughout the earth. These initial coverts are the 144,000 Jews from every tribe of Israel who will receive Jesus as their Savior.

Understand, the minute the church is removed from the earth, the earth reverts back to the time of the cross where Jewish time originally stopped. At the time of the cross, Israel was a dominant force in the earth under Roman authority. Forty years following Jesus' death on the cross, everything changed. Rome was still a power, but Israel was scattered in 70 A.D. Rome increasingly degenerated during the years that followed until it disappeared as a world empire. The city of Rome still exists, but not in power as the Roman Empire once displayed. Power shifted from Rome to Gentile nations around the world and no longer was there a single dominant force. During the church age, no single world empire has existed with the exception of the church itself.

Why are Rome and Israel so important? It is because Daniel's sixty-ninth week ended when Rome was in power and Israel was under their authority. At the end of the sixty-ninth week, the church was inserted. Daniel was unaware of the church because it was a mystery. Daniel saw all of the weeks happening sequentially with no gaps in between. He honestly believed that 490 years from the time the decree was given, Messiah was coming. This is the same reason the disciples believed the kingdom was coming at any moment. By their calculations, the kingdom was at a minimum, seven years away. They were excited!

About the time the disciples believed Daniel's seventieth week was approaching, Jesus Christ appears on the scene. Jesus begins preaching about "the kingdom" and they are asking Jesus, "Can my son sit at Your right hand? Can my son sit at Your left hand? Just like the crowd, the disciples believed Jesus had come to destroy the Roman Empire and set up His eternal kingdom on earth because of Daniel's prophecy. They had no idea that after Daniel's sixty-ninth week Jewish time would be suspended for some two thousand years.

In Acts, chapter one, Jesus told His disciples, "I want you to go and wait for the Holy Spirit, for you will receive power after the Holy Ghost is come upon you to be My witnesses. You will be endued with power from on high." Jesus knew once they received the Holy Spirit, they would understand a new dispensation had begun. However, the moment Jesus finished speaking this to them, they asked, "When is the kingdom coming?" They were not interested in the Day of Pentecost, they wanted to know about the kingdom. Jesus has been raised from the dead and He has His resurrection body. What a perfect time for the kingdom to come. When they asked Him the question Jesus said, "*It is not for you to know the times or the seasons, which the Father put in His own power. But you will receive power after the Holy Ghost is come upon you. Go to Jerusalem.*" Then they stood and watched as Jesus was taken from their sight into heaven. As they watched Jesus disappear, they continued and continued watching, and suddenly two men, who were angels, stood by them in white apparel asking, "Why are you looking up?" They kept watching because they expected Jesus to reappear. The angels said, "This same Jesus you have seen go away shall come again *in like manner.*" The angels were referring to the second advent because even they did not know about the rapture yet. It was a mystery to them!

There were three Who knew about the coming of the church: The *Father*, the *Son*, and the *Holy Spirit*. The disciples did not know. The angels did not know. The demons did not know. Satan himself did not know. Even though the disciples were looking for the kingdom, they went to the upper room and when they came down from the room, a whole new dispensation had begun. Not only were the disciples surprised, Satan was surprised, demons were surprised, and the angels in heaven were looking at each other saying, "What is this? We didn't know this was on the calendar!" while God was smiling and saying,

"There has been a change of operaı
once brought revelation to, you will nı
You will attend their services and will
That is what Peter is referring to wheı
things the angels desire to look into" (1 ɾeter 1:12).

When the end of the church age is nearing, Jerusalem
and the Jews will return to a place of prominence in the
earth, Rome will rise up and the moment the church is
removed, everything reverts to the time of the cross
because God has to complete what has not been completed.
Jewish time has only been temporarily stopped; it has not
been completed.

Once the church is removed from earth, Israel will
again be under the authority of a Roman empire, but it
will be the revived Roman Empire. The leader of the
revived Roman Empire will make a covenant with Israel
for seven years. For the first three and a half years, Israel
will believe this leader is their Messiah, but in the middle
of the Tribulation he will break his covenant and treaty
with Israel and reveal himself to be the Antichrist.

How do we know the church age is coming to a close?
The first place we look is to Israel. Many Jews have
returned to Israel and many more will return when Jesus
comes for the rapture of the church. We also look to the
rise of the revived Roman Empire. Although it is has been
revised, the European Economic Community is on the
rise and becoming strong today. At the moment there are

welve nations involved but when the Tribulation begins, there will only be ten nations in the EEC.

When God stopped Jewish time at the cross, they could look into the future and see the coming of Jesus Christ, but it was in the distance. The Jews have been sitting at the stop sign for two thousand years and a day is fast approaching when God will finally say, "Okay. It is time for Jewish time to be completed." Israel will have the final seven years of Jewish time to find Jesus as their Lord and Savior.

Daniel 9:27:

And he [Anitchrist] *shall confirm the covenant with many [many Jews for seven years] for one week: and in the midst of the week [in the middle of the seven years or three and a half years] he shall cause the sacrifice and the oblation to cease...*

During the first half of the Tribulation, the Jews will believe the Antichrist is the Messiah and will receive him as such. He will make a covenant with them, promise them protection from all surrounding hostile nations. At this time, America will not be the most powerful nation on the earth; the power will shift to Europe, and Israel will have an ally with the most powerful nation in the world.

What Israel will not realize is that the leader of the revived Roman Empire will want to pull them into servitude.

What will mark the middle of the Tribulation is this leader will break his covenant with Israel and the Jewish people. He will walk into the temple in Jerusalem, sit on the throne reserved for the Messiah, command sacrifices to stop, and demand they bow down and worship him. This is when the Jews will realize that he is not the Messiah and there will be great weeping and wailing in Jerusalem. However, there will be many Christians who will understand this marks a very important day and they will flee to the mountains in obedience to God's command.

> *...and for the overspreading of abominations he shall make it desolate, even until the consummation, and that determined shall be poured out upon the desolate.*

The Antichrist, who is the desolator, will literally desecrate the temple. He will bring humiliation to the people and this will all take place during the final three and a half years of the Tribulation.

Nebuchadnezzar's Dream

Daniel, chapter two describes a horrible dream King Nebuchadnezzar had and Daniel's interpretation of that dream. King Nebuchadnezzar's dream was so horrible he woke up in a cold sweat; he could not remember the dream but he knew that it was terrible. It disturbed him so much he called for all of his magicians, astrologers, and sorcerers to find an interpretation of the dream. The king's wise men asked him to explain the dream but he could not remember it. The king told his wise men there would be great rewards for the one who could interpret the dream, but a violent death to the men and their families who could not. The wise men said, "There is no man on the face the earth who can interpret a dream if he doesn't know what the dream is!"

In his anger King Nebuchadnezzar sent forth a decree for all of the wise men to be killed. When the king's men came for Daniel because of the decree, Daniel spoke with great wisdom asking for some time so he could find the interpretation for the king. Then Daniel, Shadrach, Meshach, and Abednego sought the Lord to give the dream and the interpretation of the dream to Daniel, which He did. Daniel went to the king and said, "I'm going to give you the interpretation of the dream not to glorify me but so that you know there is a God in heaven Who knows what is in your heart." So, Daniel gave the interpretation.

Daniel 2:31-35:

Thou, O king, sawest, a behold a great image. This great image, whose brightness was excellent, stood before thee; and the form therof was terrible.

This image's head was of fine gold, his breast and his arms of silver, his belly and his thighs of brass,

His legs of iron, his feet part of iron and part of clay.

Thou sawest till that a stone was cut out without hands, which smote the image upon his feet that were of iron and clay, and brake them to pieces.

Then as the iron, the clay, the brass, the silver, and the gold, broken to pieces together, and became like the chaff of the summer threshingfloors; and the wind carried them away, that no place was found for them: and the stone that smote the image became a great mountain, and filled the whole earth.

What Daniel described was an image. The head was made of gold, the chest and arms of silver, the belly and thighs of brass, the legs of iron, and the feet of a mixture of both iron and clay. The clay being referred to is potter's clay. It has been baked and is very brittle and can break easily. Notice, there is a degeneration of substances used in the image.

The head of gold represents Babylon and the reign of Nebuchadnezzar. Nebuchadnezzar had a giant golden image built of himself. He believed he was the most important person on the face of the earth and as a result, for seven years he roamed the earth like an animal. When he finally came to the end of himself, he acknowledged God and accepted Him as the true and living God.

In Daniel chapter five, there is a transition between Babylonian rule and the Medes and Persians. The Medes and Persians represent the two arms of silver. The Medes and Persians conquered Babylon and were the next world empires that reigned. The kingdom of Babylon was conquered in one night.

The belly and thighs of brass represent the Greek Empire under Alexander the Great. Alexander conquered the entire known world in twelve years. Toward the end of Alexander's reign, his kingdom was divided into four different nations under four different kings, all striving for power.

One finally did rise up and dominate the others.

The nation that rose up in power was Rome. The two legs of iron represent the Roman Empire. The length of the legs represents the fact the Roman Empire was the longest world empire to ever exist. They ruled for over a thousand years. Jesus Christ was born during the Roman Empire.

The feet represent the revived Roman Empire and the time of the Tribulation. When the Roman Empire is revived, it will not have the same power it once had. The entire world is represented in the iron and clay of the feet. The iron is the revived Roman Empire and the clay represents all other nations of the world. People often ask, "Where will the United States be in all of this?" It is one of the clay nations. During the Tribulation, America will no longer be the power it currently is in the world today. All emphasis will shift to Rome in regard to world domination.

Note, iron and clay do not mix well. If they do mix, it is a very fragile relationship. Teaching that says Rome will control the entire world is not true. Rome will try to dominate but there will be nations against them throughout the Tribulation. There will be very loose control as they try to dominate the world.

Probably the most fragile part of the body represented in the image is the feet. Without the feet, getting from one place to another becomes very difficult without some type of assistance.

In verse 34, Daniel describes a stone *"cut out without hands."* The stone is Jesus Christ. Being *"cut out without hands"* represents the virgin birth. This stone will strike the image on the feet and because the clay is so brittle, the image will topple to the ground completely destroyed. After the image is destroyed, the stone, Jesus, will rise up and the reign of the Lord will cover the entire earth. The thousand year reign of Jesus Christ will begin at this time.

The church is found between the legs and feet. For 2,000 years an empire has existed called "the church." Daniel did not see it in the image because the church is part of the mystery. Daniel saw the entire image flowing together, one nation's dominion following another. He did not understand the church would be inserted before the Tribulation.

The Four Great Beasts

Daniel 7:1-8:

In the first year of Balshazzar king of Babylon Daniel had a dream and visions of his head upon his bed: then he wrote the dream, and told the sum of the matters.

Daniel spake and said, I saw in my vision by night, and, behold, the four winds of the heaven strove upon the great sea.

And four great beasts came up from the sea, diverse one from another.

The first was like a lion, and had eagle's wings: I
beheld, and lo another, like a leopard, which had
upon the back of it four wings of a fowl; the beast had
also four heads; and dominion was given to it.

And behold another beast, a second, like to a bear,
and it raised up itself on one side, and it had three
ribs in the mouth of it between the teeth of it: and
they said thus unto it, Arise, devour much flesh.

After this I beheld, and lo another, like a leopard,
which had upon the back of it four wings of a fowl;
the beast had also four heads; and dominion was
given to it.

After this I saw in the night visions, and behold
a fourth beast, dreadful and terrible, and strong
exceedingly; and it had great iron teeth: it devoured
and brake in pieces, and stamped the residue with the
feet of it: and it was diverse from all the beasts that
were before it; and it had ten horns.

I considered the horns, and, behold, there came up
among them another little horn, before whom there
were three of the first horns plucked up by the roots:
and, behold, in this horn were eyes like the eyes of
man, and a mouth speaking great things.

The "four winds of the heaven" is the moving of history. Nations conquering nations, war, times changing; God is in control of nations and history. The "great sea" represents all the Gentile nations of the earth. The beasts described can be compared to the different parts of the image described in Daniel, chapter two.

The first beast described was like a lion with wings. This is Babylon during the reign of Nebuchadnezzar, which was a rapidly rising empire. The lion is the king of the beasts and a very strong animal. With wings, the lion is not only strong, it is also quick. This beast represents a strong nation rising rapidly to power.

The second beast was like a bear that raised itself up and had three ribs in its mouth. This beast represents the Medes and Persians and the three ribs represent the divisions of the different nations conquered.

Alexander the Great and the Greek Empire are represented by the third beast. It is like a leopard but it too, has wings. A leopard is known for its speed and with wings it would be a very fast creature. This beast represents how rapidly Alexander rose to power and conquered all the nations of the known world.

Alexander was brilliant and one of the few true geniuses in history. Very few geniuses are ever born. Alexander understood that to conquer the entire world, there would need to be a common language. In a very short time, Alexander invented a language called koine Greek.

"Koine" means "common." Alexander invented a street language. Not like the flowery Greek that had existed before Homeric Greek or classic Greek. He created a language the average person could understand and he taught it to his army and the entire nation. Each time his armies would conquer a nation they would force that nation to learn the koine Greek. By the time Jesus Christ came into the earth, every nation of the world was bilingual and every nation could speak koine Greek. God inspired Alexander to create the koine Greek language in preparation for the writing of the New Testament so the gospel could be taken to the entire world. The disciples could go from nation to nation speaking koine Greek and everyone could understand. This language is not a supernatural one, but the formation of it was. God ordained it and used an unbeliever to cause it to come to pass. Alexander was an unbeliever, died an unbeliever, died an alcoholic but God used his brilliance to bring about the koine Greek and rapid conquering of the world. It is incredible to think in just twelve years the entire world spoke the same language!

The fourth beast is given no name because Daniel has never seen a beast that looks like this one. This beast will represent Rome and the revived Romans Empire. In describing the fourth beast Daniel says, "*...and behold a fourth beast, dreadful and terrible, and strong exceedingly; and it had great iron teeth.*" Notice, iron is mentioned again, representing Rome.

The verse continues, "*...it devoured and brake in pieces, and stamped the residue with the feet of it.*" It was common for Rome to destroy a nation they had conquered. They would return and plow it under, adding insult to injury. After plowing the nation under, they would often pour salt on the ground to prevent it from producing. Not only did they devour the nation, the stamped it out with their feet; "*...it was diverse from all the beasts that were before it; and it had ten horns.*" This beast is different than the previous beasts because it diminishes as a world power but then rises again.

Verse eight continues, "*I considered the horns, and, behold, there came up among them another little horn, before whom there were three of the first horns plucked up by the roots: and, behold, in this horn were eyes like the eyes of man, and a mouth speaking great things.*"

The beast is described as having ten horns. The ten horns represent ten nations of the revived Roman Empire. There were ten toes on the image described in Daniel two, also representing the ten nations. The "little horn" that rises up is the Anitchrist. The Antichrist will immediately destroy three nations, which will probably establish his power in the EEC.

Daniel 7:9:

*I beheld till the thrones were cast down, and the
Ancient of days did sit, whose garment was white as
snow, and the hair of his head like the pure wool:
his throne was like the fiery flame, and his wheels as
burning fire.*

The "Ancient of days" is the also the "stone cut without
hands," Jesus Christ Who will one day soon, sit upon the
throne and rule the entire world. It is good to know we do
not need to fear the Antichrist because we are serving the
Lord of the universe, our Lord Jesus Christ!

6

The Temple Discourse

The First Palm Sunday

The book of Matthew is the greatest of the four gospels in teaching the end times. Matthew presents Jesus Christ as the king of the Jews both in His day and the time to come. To be the king of the Jews, He must be eligible to sit on the throne. Palm Sunday is described by Matthew when the people realize Jesus is their King, their Messiah.

Matthew 21:8-9:

> *And a very great multitude spread their garments in the way; others cut down branches from the trees, and strawed them in the way.*

> *And the multitudes that went before, and that followed, cried, saying, Hosanna to the son of David: Blessed is he that cometh in the name of the Lord; Hosanna in the highest.*

The word "Hosanna" is a Hebrew word brought into the Greek and it means "prosperity." The people are crying for prosperity. The phrase *"Blessed is he that cometh in the name of the Lord"* is a quote from the Old Testament. Why were the crowds shouting this in the streets? They were quoting Psalm 118 in which David was speaking prophetically.

The Stone Which the Builders Rejected

Psalm 118:21-24:

> *I will praise thee: for thou hast heard me, and art become my salvation.*

> *The stone which the builders refused is become the head stone of the corner.*

> *This is the Lord's doing; it is marvelous in our eyes.*

> *This is the day which the Lord hath made; we will rejoice and be glad in it.*

David is seeing Jesus Christ as his salvation. These verses are first advent scriptures. This is Jesus coming to earth, living and walking in the earth for thirty years, being baptized in the River Jordan, performing three years of signs, wonders, and miracles, and finally going to the cross. He has become our salvation!

The "stone" is Jesus and the "builders" are the Jews, especially the religious Jews. Many Jews received Jesus, but many did not. The religious leaders hated and despised Him. He is the stone the builders rejected, but after they rejected Him He became the head of the corner. The corner He has become the head of is the church. After being rejected by the Jews, Jesus arose from the dead and became the cornerstone upon which everything in our dispensation is built. In other words, Psalm 118 is actually prophetic concerning the coming of the Church. We are told in I Peter 2:5, *"Ye also, as lively (living) stones, are built up a spiritual house, an holy priesthood, to offer up spiritual sacrifices, acceptable to God by Jesus Christ."* Jesus said, in Matthew 16:18, *"...I will build my church; and the gates of hell will not prevail against it."*

Verse 24 of Psalm 118 says again, *"This is the day which the Lord has made; we will be glad and rejoice in it."* The *"day"* being referred to is the day of salvation, which was accomplished through the cross, by the death, burial, and resurrection of Jesus Christ.

Verse 25 continues, *"Save now, I beseech thee, O Lord: O Lord, I beseech thee, send now prosperity."* The phrase *"save now"* is the Hebrew word for *"Hosanna."* It is a second advent verse, which is connected by *"Hosanna... send now prosperity."* The sending of prosperity is during the millennial reign of Jesus Christ.

The timetable again, is the Rapture will occur and the church will end. The Tribulation will begin and last for seven years, which is synonymous with Daniel's seventieth week. The Second Advent will occur at the end of the Tribulation and the Millennium will begin and last for a thousand years. The Millennium will be a time of economic worldwide prosperity. At the Second Advent, people will be crying "Hosanna! Hosanna! Bring now prosperity!" The church will not be crying, but those believers on earth who will have been through the Battle of Armageddon will be. They will be shouting for deliverance and He will deliver them and bring worldwide prosperity.

Verse 26 of Psalm 118 continues, *"Blessed is he that cometh in the name of the Lord: we have blessed you out of the house of the Lord."* This is referring to the Tribulational temple and the Millennial temple that is yet to be built.

Exactly what happened in Matthew twenty-one? Jesus is riding into town on a donkey, about to go to the cross, and the people are throwing palm leaves in front of Him on the road and shouting, *"Hosanna, save us now! Bring now prosperity! Blessed is He that cometh in the name of the Lord!"*

The crowds were shouting the second part of the prophecy and not the first part. They left out, *"...the stone which the builders rejected has become the head of the corner. This is the Lord's doing. It is marvelous in our eyes. This is the day the Lord has made for us to rejoice and be glad!"* The people skipped over this entire section and began crying, *"Hosanna! Hosanna! Blessed is He that cometh in the name of the Lord!"*

A few days later, Jesus went to the cross. He had not conquered the Roman Empire and He had not set up His kingdom. The same group of people yelled, *"Crucify Him! Crucify Him! Crucify Him!"* These were not believers shouting; these were people in the street trying to usher in the second advent. They wanted the crown without the cross, but no one can have the crown without going to the cross first. No one can rule and reign with Jesus Christ without first becoming a born again believer. The people were wanting all of the benefits of the cross without accepting Jesus Christ as their Lord and Savior.

Parable of the Evil Husbandmen

After riding into the Jerusalem (Matthew 21), Jesus entered the temple. Most of Matthew chapters 21, 22, and 23 take place in the temple. Prior to this time, Jesus had spent very little time in the temple. The first time He entered the temple, he threw out the moneychangers. When He entered the temple again, He began addressing the religious leaders.

Matthew 21:33-40:

Hear another parable: There was a certain householder, which planted a vineyard, and hedged it round about, and digged a winepress in it, and built a tower, and let it out to husbandmen, and went into a far country:

And when the time of the fruit drew near, he sent his servants to the husbandmen, that they might receive the fruits of it.

And the husbandmen took his servants, and beat one, and killed another, and stoned another.

Again, he sent other servants more than the first: and they did unto them likewise.

But last of all he sent unto them his son, saying, They will reverence my son.

But when the husbandmen saw the son, they said among themselves, This is the heir; come, let us kill him, and let us seize on his inheritance.

And they caught him, and cast him out of the vineyard, and slew him.

When the lord therefore of the vineyard cometh, what will he do unto those husbandmen?

The husbandmen are the Jews, the Pharisees. God had given them the nation of Israel, but Israel is more than a nation. They were given the gospel. The fruit of the winepress represents the gospel. The Jews were to spread the gospel, but they did not do it. This was their purpose from the time of the Old Testament. The owner sent his servants representing the Old Testament prophets— Zechariah, Jeremiah, Isaiah—all of the prophets found in the Old Testament. But the husbandmen beat, stoned, and even killed some of the servants.

Finally, the owner (God) said, "That's it. The last one I will send is my own son." The husbandmen said, "This is the heir. Let's seize and kill him and then we'll get the inheritance."

As Jesus shared the story, the religious leaders were becoming angry with the husbandmen. They did not yet realize that Jesus was referring to them as He told the story. Jesus finally asked them what would be proper to do to the husbandmen.

Matthew 21:41:

They say unto him, He will miserably destroy those wicked men, and will let out his vineyard unto other

*husbandmen, which shall render him the fruits in
their seasons.*

The Pharisees tell Jesus, "If the owner is smart, he
will take the vineyard from the husbandmen and give it to
someone who really cares."

Matthew 21:43-46:

*Jesus saith unto them, Did ye never read in the
scriptures, The stone which the builders rejected, the
same is become the head of the corner: this is the
Lord's doing, and it is marvelous in our eyes?*

*Therefore say I unto you, The kingdom of God shall
be taken from you, and given to a nation bringing
forth the fruits thereof.*

*And whosoever shall fall on this stone shall be
broken: but on whomsoever it shall fall, it will grind
him to powder.*

*And when the chief priests and Pharisees had heard
his parables, they perceived that he spake of them.*

But when they sought to lay hands on him, they feared the multitude, because they took him for a prophet.

In essence, Jesus said, "I am the stone and you are the ones who will reject me." Immediately, the fulfillment of the prophecy looked eminent. The religious leaders would have killed Him but feared the reaction of the crowds.

Notice, Jesus quoted the verses from Psalm 118 which the crowds did not quote. Instead, they bypassed the cross and went immediately to the Second Advent. Jesus told the religious leaders and multitudes, "I am not here to bring *'Hosanna! Hosanna! Blessed is He that comes in the name of the Lord.'* I'm not here to *'...save now, save now!'* I am here to be the stone which the builders rejected. *Then* I'm going to rise from the dead and become the head of the corner. I am going to become the head of a whole new generation, a whole new kingdom which will exist for a long time. Then one day you can shout, *'Hosanna! Hosanna! Blessed is He that comes in the name of the Lord.'"*

Jesus Confronts the Religious Leaders

In Matthew 23, Jesus confronts the religious leaders. Until this time, He has tried to avoid them and confronted them on an individual basis. Now Jesus, before a multitude, addresses an entire group of religious leaders.

Matthew 23:23:

> *Woe unto you, scribes and Pharisees, hypocrites! For ye pay tithe of mint and anise and cumin, and have omitted the weightier matters of the law, judgment, mercy, and faith: these ought ye to have done, and not to leave the other undone.*

Jesus is simply saying, "You made mountains out of molehills. You made the people pay tithes on the smallest things—spices—and omitted the most important parts of the law." The law did teach tithing but it also taught judgment, mercy, and faith which the scribes and Pharisees neglected to teach the people.

Matthew 23:24:

> *Ye blind guides, which strain at a gnat, and swallow a camel.*

These religious leaders were experts on the law, even down to the minutest detail. The people were waiting to hear about love, justice, mercy, and faith. But all they were receiving was "Pay your tithe of mint. Pay your tithe of anise. Pay your tithe of cumin. We haven't seen your cinnamon. We haven't seen your nutmeg. Give it! Pay!" The scribes and Pharisees majored on the least significant aspects of the law and neglected to teach the major areas of the Word.

Matthew 23:25:

> *Woe unto you, scribes and Pharisees, hypocrites! for ye make clean the outside of the cup and the platter, but within they are full of extortion and excess!*

The religious leaders were guilty of two things: *extortion* and *excess.* They were extorting money from the people and spending it on themselves. It is common to find crime hidden behind the façade of religion. Jesus was saying, "Behind the walls of religion is crime. You have cleaned up the outside of the cup, but inside, the cup is filled with extortions and excess."

Matthew 23:26:

> *Thou blind Pharisee, cleanse first that which is within the cup and platter, that the outside of them may be clean also.*

Jesus is simply telling them, "Receive Jesus as Lord and Savior. First, clean up your heart—that which is inside—and then your actions (the outside) will follow.

Matthew 23:27:

> *Woe unto you scribes and Pharisees, hypocrites! for ye are like unto whited sepulchers, which indeed appear beautiful outward, but are within full of dead men's bones, and of all uncleanness.*

What a perfect description of religion: whitewashed and beautiful on the outside but filled with death on the inside.

Matthew 23:28-32:

> *Even so ye also outwardly appear righteous unto men, but within ye are full of hypocrisy and iniquity.*

> *Woe unto you, scribes and Pharisees, hypocrites! because ye build the tombs of the prophets, and garnish the sepulchers of the righteous,*

> *And say, If we had been in the days of our fathers, we would not have been partakers with them in the blood of the prophets.*

Wherefore ye be witnesses unto yourselves, that ye are the children of them which killed the prophets.

Fill ye up then the measure of your fathers.

Jesus confronts them, "You tell us if you had lived in the time of your fathers you would not have killed the prophets, but mark it down, you are the children of your fathers. Your fathers filled a portion of the cup with the blood of the prophets who were martyred, but you will fill the cup full. Your fathers killed the prophets, but you are going to kill the One the prophets prophesied of; you're going to kill the Messiah and fill the cup to overflowing.

Matthew 23:33-34:

Ye serpents, ye generation of vipers, how can ye escape the damnation of hell?

Wherefore, behold, I send unto you prophets, and wise men, and scribes: and some of them ye shall kill and crucify; and some of them shall ye scourge in your synagogues, and persecute them from city to city:

Verse 34 is a prophecy about the church. Jesus is describing to them what is to come. "You will kill Me and once the church begins, you will chase believers from city to city and scourge and beat them. You're going to do it in the synagogues!" This verse is a perfect description of what Saul did before his conversion. He led many to persecute the church in an attempt to destroy it before becoming the apostle Paul.

Matthew 23:35-38:

That upon you may come all the righteous blood shed upon the earth, from the blood of righteous Abel unto the blood of Zacharias son of Barachias, whom ye slew between the temple and the altar.

Verily I say unto you, All these things shall come upon this generation.

O Jerusalem, Jerusalem, thou that killest the prophets, and stonest them which are sent unto thee, how often would I have gathered thy children together, even as a hen gathereth her chickens under her wings, and ye would not!

Behold, you house is left unto you desolate.

Both the temple and the city will be destroyed in 70 AD.

Matthew 23:39:

*For I say unto you, Ye shall not see me henceforth,
till ye shall say, Blessed is he that cometh in the name
of the Lord.*

Jesus finished what the religious leaders should have
said. Again, He told them, "One day there will be a
remnant of your children who will cry, *'Hosanna! Blessed
is he that comes in the name of the Lord!'* but you will
not see Me again until that day. Israel, you had your
chance. Pharisees, you had your chance. Jerusalem, you
had your chance. How often would I have taken you under
My wing if you would have just received the prophecy
and received Me! Instead, you will kill Me and persecute
believers. From synagogue to synagogue, city to city you
will chase them down and kill them. The opportunity you
have had extended toward you is being removed and given
to another nation."

Jesus Departs from the Temple

Matthew 24:1 says, *"And Jesus went out, and departed
from the temple..."* Notice, two statements are made: *He
went out. He departed.* Instead of simply saying, "Jesus
left the temple," the statement is divided into two parts.
The reason for the two parts is Jesus departed from the

temple and never returned. Jesus spoke His peace and departed.

The verse continues, *"...and his disciples came to him for to show him the buildings of the temple."* Understand, the disciples did not understand the significance of what Jesus had just spoken. Jesus did not have twelve super-spiritual men following Him; He had people just like you and me! After going through His discourse, the disciples came to Jesus and said, "Did you notice the temple buildings? Aren't they impressive!"

Matthew 24:2-3:

> *And Jesus said unto them, See ye not all these things? Verily I say unto you, There shall not be left here one stone upon another, that shall not be thrown down.*

> *And as they sat upon the mount of Olives, the disciples came unto him privately, saying, Tell us, when shall these things be? And what shall be the sign of they coming, and of the end of the world?*

Jesus now prophesies the destruction of the temple, which will occur less than forty years from that date. He prophesied, "What Daniel spoke of is coming to pass. Messiah will be cut off, and a flood will come in, which is *'the people of the prince that is yet to come.'"* The *"people of the prince that is yet to come"* surrounded Jesus. The streets were filled with Romans and Jesus continued, "See this place? Not one stone will be left on another."

The disciples were excited. They said to Jesus, "This is what we have been waiting for. Thank You, Jesus! When will these things be? What will be the sign of Your coming? What will be the sign of the end of the age?"

The disciples asked Jesus three questions. Jesus answered all three. We need to understand where the disciples were coming from. When they asked about the end of the "age" they were referring to the Jewish age. They did not understand the church age, it was a mystery. The end of the Jewish age is Daniel's seventieth week or the Tribulation. Jesus will begin to describe the Tribulation in the verses that follow. The disciples did not know to ask about the end of the church age. In their thinking, they are seven years away from the millennial reign of Jesus Christ. In chapters 24 and 25, known as the Olivet Discourse, Jesus will describe what will happen during the Tribulation and at His second coming.

7

The Tribulation

The Olivet Discourse

The book of Matthew contains more from the teaching ministry of Jesus than any of the four gospels. It contains the *Sermon on the Mount* (chapters 5-7), the *kingdom parables* (chapter 13), the *Temple Discourse* (chapters 21-23), and the *Olivet Discourse* (chapters 24-25).

The *Olivet Discourse* takes place on the Mount of Olives. The three other gospels record segments of this sermon, but Matthew records the sermon almost in its entirety. To understand this passage it is important to understand that Matthew 24 and 25 are presented in chronological order. A chapter separation was not necessary between the chapters. Matthew 25 is simply a continuation of the very same sermon.

Matthew 24:1:

> *And Jesus went out, and departed from the temple: and his disciples came to him for to show him the buildings of the temple.*

As mentioned previously, the disciples were greatly impressed with the beauty of the temple. It was considered one of the seven wonders of the ancient world. The temple of Solomon had been destroyed and when the children of Israel returned from their captivity, they rebuilt the temple. Zechariah, Nahum, and other Old Testament prophets gave an account of this in their writings. When the temple was rebuilt, it was smaller than Solomon's Temple. Because the younger people had not seen the old temple, the size was insignificant to them, but the older people were very upset about the size.

They remembered the size of Solomon's temple and were discouraged because the rebuilt temple was not as large. From the time the temple was rebuilt, it had been improved and expanded over the years. King Herod invested vast sums of money into the temple trying to persuade the Jews to support him, but because Herod was not a Jew and was hired by the Romans to sit on the throne, the Jews hated him. Though the Jews hated Herod, they loved the beauty of the temple. As the disciples were gazing upon the buildings of the temple, they pointed out the beauty of them to Jesus saying, "Jesus, have you ever really looked at this temple?" And as Jesus looked He responded, "Go ahead and take one last look because it won't be long before not one stone will remain upon another."

Matthew 24:2:

And Jesus said unto them, See ye not all these things?
verily I say unto you, There shall not be left here one
stone upon another, that shall not be thrown down.

The moment Jesus finished speaking, the disciples were filled with fear immediately followed by excitement. They became fearful because Jesus spoke openly in the streets of the destruction of the temple while being surrounded by both Romans and Jews who believed Jesus was a rebel.

Their excitement came because the disciples understood Old Testament prophesies concerning the Second Coming of Jesus Christ. They realized they were coming to the end of 483 years and were close to the completion of Daniel's seventy weeks. Because of their excitement, the disciples led Jesus away from the crowds to the Mount of Olives and then bombarded Him with questions.

The Disciples Question Jesus

Matthew 24:3:

And as he sat upon the mount of Olives, the disciples
came unto him privately, saying, Tell us, when shall
these things be? And what shall be the sign of thy
coming, and of the end of the world?

The word "world" is the Greek word "aion" meaning "age." Some translations render this phrase, "What is the sign of the end of the age?" Notice, the disciples did not ask Jesus one question, they asked Him three questions.

Question number one: When shall these things be?

Question number two: What will be the sign of thy coming?

Question number three: What will be the sign of the end of the age?

The disciples did not give Jesus time to answer their questions, they simply exploded with one question after another. Jesus answered all three questions, however the answer to question number one is not found in Matthew; it is found in the gospel of Luke.

Luke 21:20-24:

And when you shall see Jerusalem compassed with armies, then know the desolation thereof is nigh.

Then let them which are in Judaea flee to the mountains; and let them which are in the midst of it depart out; and let not them that are in the countries enter thereinto.

For these be the days of vengeance, that all things which are written may be fulfilled.

But woe unto them that are with child, and to them that give suck, in those days! for there shall be great distress in the land, and wrath upon this people.

And they shall fall by the edge of the sword, and shall be led away captive into all nations: and Jerusalem shall be trodden down of the Gentiles, until the time of the Gentiles be fulfilled.

When Jesus said "you," He was addressing the disciples. He was telling them, "This will happen in your lifetime. Look for Jerusalem to be surrounded by armies." Daniel described who these armies would be. He described them as the "people of the prince that is yet to come" and was referring to the Romans. Daniel did not call them "Romans" because the Romans were not yet in existence at the time of his prophecy.

The armies of Rome surrounded the city of Jerusalem. The first thing they did was cut off food, water, and supplies from the children of Israel. They starved the Jews to weaken them. Some of the most horrendous things took place. Because the people were starving, their priorities were completely turned around. Rather than seeing their children as precious, they were viewed as their parents' next meal. The Jews were slaying and eating their own children. Josephus records they were eating anything made of leather; they were also eating rats so they could survive. This is how desperate their situation had become. As soon as a person died, they grabbed the body and separated it for food.

After the Jews had become so weak they could not defend themselves, the Romans came into the city and attacked. They began to kill and slay people and any survivors were taken captive and scattered throughout the world.

Some Jews knew and believed Daniel's prophecy and the moment they saw Jerusalem compassed with armies, they fled. Jesus was exhorting the disciples, "If you are wise and know the Word, as soon as you see the armies begin to surround Jerusalem, you will find a way to flee the city as quickly as possible."

Luke 21:24 again says, "...*Jerusalem will be trodden down by the Gentiles, until the time of the Gentiles is fulfilled.*" The Gentiles being referred to are the Romans. The Romans compassed Jerusalem in 70 AD and the entire city was destroyed. The temple was destroyed. Many people died and others were led away captive. The *"time of the Gentiles"* is the church age. Jerusalem will be under the feet of Gentile nations until the church age ends.

We live in very exciting times. In 1948, Israel was re-inhabited. In 1966, they reoccupied the city of Jerusalem. The time of the Gentiles is very near to being fulfilled. Jesus warns of a day that parallels the destruction of Jerusalem by the Romans, which will occur right before the Second Coming of Jesus Christ.

The second question the disciples posed was "What will be the sign of Your coming?" The answer to this question is found in verses 27-51 of Matthew twenty-four. The "coming" to which the disciples are referring is the Second Coming of Jesus because as mentioned before, they did not know about the church age; it was a mystery.

Although the Tribulation will not begin until the church is gone from the earth, there will be indicators of the Tribulation while the church is still on the earth. Small waves are hitting today as precursors to the tidal wave of the Tribulation. John indicated this would be the case when he said, "Before the Antichrist comes, you will see many antichrists—people who represent the Antichrist. The Bible says that the mystery of iniquity is already at work.

The answer to question number three is found in Matthew 24, verses 9 through twenty-six.

Matthew 24:4:

And Jesus answered and said unto them, Take heed that no man deceive you.

Beware of Deception

The way to be certain no man deceive you, is to know the Word of God. Ignorance of the Word leads to deception. Deception is not a lie; it is a lie mixed with the truth. It begins with the truth so the listener is in agreement with what is being said, and then a lie is inserted. When deception enters, it becomes difficult to discern where the truth ended and the lie began. If a person wanted to poison a dog, they would hide the poison in a piece of meat; they would hide it in something that is good. That is exactly how people fall for deception. False teachers take a promise of God, add something false, or twist an interpretation of the scripture. Do not ever let anyone tell you that you are reading or studying the Word too much. Never allow people to tell you that you are becoming "Word-bound." We can never have too much of the Word of God. We are told to meditate it day and night. That is when the Word will protect us, lead us, show us the path for our lives, bring prosperity, and bring wisdom. The importance of the Word cannot be overemphasized.

Matthew 24:5:

For many shall come in my name, saying, I am Christ; and shall deceive many.

We have many false Christ's in the world today. They profess to be the "Anointed One". Others will come who will say, "Jesus was the Messiah for past generations; but I am the Messiah for your generation. I have been sent by God."

Knowing the Word of God is essential to recognizing false religion and deception. The Word in your heart will guide you in identifying erroneous teaching. Error cannot withstand the truth of God's Word.

Wars and Rumors of Wars

Matthew 24:6:

And ye shall hear of wars and rumours of wars: see that ye be not troubled: for all these things must come to pass, but the end is not yet.

The wars we are seeing in the earth today are leading up to the greatest war that will ever come—the Battle of Armageddon. Two types of wars are mentioned: *wars* and *rumors* of wars. Wars are wars that are actually taking place. Rumors of wars are cold wars.

Notice, verse 6 says "all these things **must** come to pass." Understand there will never be peace in the earth until the Prince of Peace returns. Many become involved in efforts to bring peace into the earth, but Christians should not get caught up in these efforts. Instead, we are to be involved in spreading the gospel of Jesus Christ. Jesus will bring peace to the earth at the Second Coming. Jesus said when we hear of wars and rumors of wars we are not to be disturbed because these things must come to pass.

The United Nations will not bring peace to the world. Although their mission may sound noble and good, they cannot bring world peace. It is interesting that a scripture is posted outside the United Nations that says, "They will beat their swords into plowshares and their spears into pruninghooks," but there are verses that precede and follow this verse. The UN will not fulfill this scripture; Jesus will. Men may do everything humanly possible to unite together, as they did at the Tower of Babel, but the end will be destruction.

Matthew 24:7-8:

For nation shall rise against nation, and kingdom against kingdom: and there shall be famines, and pestilences, and earthquakes, in divers places.

All these are the beginning of sorrows.

There is a difference between nations and kingdoms. Nations are actual countries warring against one another. Kingdoms are religions battling one another. This could be Judaism against Islam. We are seeing wars of nation against nation. We are seeing wars of kingdom against kingdom.

Jesus goes on to say, "*...there shall be famines, and pestilences, and earthquakes, in divers places.*" We have seen famine in our day. We have seen pestilence—swarms of insects eating crops. There have been many earthquakes throughout the world. Jesus said, "All of these are the beginning of sorrows."

The word for "sorrows" in the Greek is "birth pangs." Jesus is telling us when we hear of wars and rumors of wars, when we see famines, pestilences, and earthquakes in the earth, the earth is getting ready to deliver. The earth is pregnant with the millennial reign of the Lord Jesus Christ. The closer we get to the point of delivery the closer will be the birth pangs of that delivery.

When a woman is getting close to her delivery time, she will have labor pains. These pains are labor pains that will birth the child. Just before the Tribulation, the earth will experience these labor pains, but when the Tribulation begins the pains will be close together and delivery will take place. Jesus will come to the earth to rule.

Romans 8:20:

> *For the creature was made subject to vanity, not willingly, but by reason of him who hath subjected the same in hope...*

The King James Version uses the word "creature" but it is actually the word "creation." Creation refers to the earth, the animals, the plants—everything that is living. The "creation was made subject to vanity." Vanity is the curse that entered the earth at the time Adam sinned. When he sinned, a curse came into the dust of the ground and everything made of dust received the curse. The part of man that received the curse is the body because it is the only part of man made from the dust. Man's body carries the curse because it comes from the dust of the ground.

Notice the verse continues saying that the creation was subjected to the curse, but "not willingly." Nature was not asked if it wanted the curse; it simply was subjected to the curse. However, there is hope for all creation and that hope is the return of Jesus Christ.

Matthew 24:9-10:

> *Then shall they deliver you up to be afflicted, and shall kill you: and ye shall be hated of all nations for my name's sake.*

154

And then shall many be offended, and shall betray one another, and shall hate one another.

Just as during World War II the Jews were pressured by the enemy to betray one another, during the Tribulation the same thing will occur.

Matthew 24:11:

And many false prophets shall rise, and shall deceive many.

This verse tells us that many will be deceived because of false prophets who will rise up during the Tribulation. As mentioned previously, the only way to be deceived at this time is through ignorance of the Word of God.

Lawlessness

Matthew 24:12:

And because iniquity shall abound, the love of many shall wax cold.

The word for "iniquity" means "lawlessness." We are already seeing lawlessness abound in our day, but it is nothing compared to what will occur during the Tribulation.

On every major television station we see programs portraying immorality as a standard. Foul language, premarital sex, homosexuality, adultery, and a disregard for authority have escalated and are considered acceptable for standard prime time television. In our schools we also see lawlessness in students who have no respect for authority and many times are in defiance of authority. Premarital sex, teenage pregnancy, and drug abuse no longer shock us because they are so prevalent among young people today. Lawlessness abounds but will reach a climax during the Tribulation. During that time multitudes will be in rebellion.

The word for "love" in verse 12 is "agape" and is referring to all those who will become believers during the Tribulation. Unless these believers stay in the Word of God, the pressure of the lawlessness around them will cause them to "wax cold."

The phrase "wax cold" is an Old English term for "turning cold." Think of a candle with melted wax. When you blow out the candle, the liquid wax gradually begins to harden. This is what the heart is being compared to in verse 12; it does not harden immediately. It waxes cold.

Enduring Until the End

Matthew 24:13:

> *But he that shall endure unto the end, the same shall be saved.*

The "end" Jesus is referring to is the end of the Tribulation. The only way Christians will endure to the end of the Tribulation is by knowing the Word of God. This verse does not mean that unless a person endures to the end he cannot be saved. The word "saved" means "spared." This verse is saying that the Christian who stands on the Word of God until the end of the Tribulation will be spared to go into the millennial reign of Jesus Christ. Multiplied millions will be born again during the Tribulation, but just as the day in which we live, believers will need to study the Word, meditate the Word, stand on the Word, and live by the Word. The Word is what will enable them to endure to the end of the Tribulation. Believers who survive the Tribulation will enter the Millennium and have children. Longevity will be restored and people will live even to the age of a thousand! There will be a great population explosion. All of these things will transpire for those who were saved during the Tribulation and survive the Second Coming of Jesus.

Many Christians will suffer martyrdom needlessly during the Tribulation because they allow the lawlessness of the world to enter into their lives, their love waxes cold, and they ultimately die prematurely. Some will die as true martyrs for the Lord, but others will die because of ignorance of the Word of God.

Matthew 24:14:

*And this gospel of the kingdom shall be preached in
all the world for a witness unto all nations; and then
shall the end come.*

Verse 14 is not a church age verse. Until the church
is removed from the earth, we preach the gospel of the
church, Jesus Christ. We are part of the church. We are part
of the body of Christ. We are part of the bride of Christ,
but during the Tribulation they will preach the gospel of
the kingdom, which is the coming millennial kingdom.

This verse says, after the gospel of the kingdom is
preached in all the world, the end will come. This is not
referring to the end of the church age, because it was a
mystery. It is referring to the end of the Tribulation.

Evangelism During the Tribulation

During the Tribulation, evangelism will occur in four
ways. There will be four massive sweeps and the gospel
will go from zero to worldwide in a period of seven years.
The Tribulation is divided into two periods of three and a
half years. During the first half of the Tribulation, 144,000
Jews will be saved, 12,000 from each of the twelve tribes
of Israel. This is found in Revelation, chapter seven. This
will be the first sweep of evangelism that occurs.

The second sweep of evangelism will be a result of the 144,000 tribulational saints witnessing in the world. This is found in Revelation 14, verses twelve and thirteen.

The third sweep of evangelism will occur during the second half of the Tribulation. It will be through the two witnesses. They will not only minister by preaching, they will also minister by mighty signs and wonders. This is found in verses one through fourteen of Revelation, chapter eleven.

The final sweep of evangelism will occur in a way that has not happened since Old Testament times—angels will preach the gospel. This is found in Revelation 14, verses six and seven. Angels do not function in this capacity during the church age. During the church age, angels are taught by man. Peter says the angels desire to look into the things we look into. The reason angels will once again preach during the Tribulation is because the earth will revert back to Jewish time. During Old Testament times, angels preached, taught, and instructed. Both Ezekiel and Zechariah had angels that instructed them and taught them things from heaven.

There are differing views on who the two witnesses will be. Most agree that Elijah is one of the witnesses. People are divided, however, on whether the second witness will be Enoch or Moses. Many believe it will be Enoch because like Elijah, he was raptured. The Bible indicates that neither of them saw death.

There is no argument that Elijah will be one of the witnesses. Malachi 4:5 says, *"Behold, I will send you Elijah the prophet before the coming of the great and dreadful day of the Lord."*

Going back one verse it says, *"Remember ye the law of Moses my servant, which I commanded unto him in Horeb for all Israel, with the statutes and judgments."* Notice, Moses is mentioned just before Elijah is mentioned. Moses represents the Word of God and Elijah represents the Holy Spirit—the two sources of the power of God in the earth.

Matthew 16:28:

Verily I say unto you, There be some standing here, which shall not taste of death, till they see the Son of man coming in his kingdom.

The "some" Jesus was referring to were Peter, James, and John. Jesus did not mean the actual Second Advent was going to occur in their day. He simply meant that they would have a preview of the Second Coming. Peter, James, and John would see Jesus as He will appear at the Second Advent.

Matthew 17:1-2:

And after six days Jesus taketh Peter, James, and John his brother, and bringeth them up into an high mountain apart,

And was transfigured before them: and his face did shine as the sun, and his raiment was white as the light.

This is a description of what Jesus will look like when He returns at the Second Advent. Jesus is going to come back as lightning from the east to the west. He will be clothed with the Shekinah glory of God.

Matthew 17:3:

And, behold, there appeared unto them Moses and Elias talking with him.

As Jesus is giving Peter, James, and John a preview of the Second Coming, the two witnesses appear. And the two that appear with Jesus are Moses and Elijah. Revelation 11 gives a description of the two witnesses.

Revelation 11:3:

> *And I will give power unto my two witnesses, and they shall prophesy a thousand two hundred and threescore days, clothed in sackcloth.*

A thousand two hundred and threescore days is equivilent to three and a half years. This will take place during the second half of the Tribulation. During that time the two witnesses will be slain and raised from the dead.

Revelation 11:4-5:

> *These are two olive trees, and the two candlesticks standing before the God of the earth* (Zechariah 4).

> *And if any man will hurt them, fire proceedeth out of their mouth, and devoureth their enemies: and if any man will hurt them, he must in this manner be killed.*

Verse 5 says that if anyone defies the two witnesses, fire will destroy them. Fire will come out of the mouths of the witnesses and destroy anyone who opposes them.

Revelation 11:6: These have power to shut heaven, that it rain not in the days of their prophecy:

In the Old Testament, the man who stopped rain from falling for three and a half years was Elijah.

> *...and have power over waters to turn them to blood, and to smite the earth with all plagues, as often as they will.*

The one who turned water to blood and smote the earth with plagues was Moses. The scriptures confirm by recounting miracles of the Old Testament, who the two witnesses will be.The two witnesses will be Moses and Elijah.

The Great Tribulation

Matthew 24:15:

> *When ye therefore shall see the abomination of desolation, spoken of by Daniel the prophet, stand in the holy place, (whoso readeth, let him understand:)*

Daniel said the abomination of desolation would occur in the middle of the week or three and a half years into the Tribulation. When Antichrist walks into the temple, sits on the throne, and demands to be worshiped. This is called the abomination of desolation.

Matthew 24:16:

Then let them which be in Judaea flee into the mountains:

When the middle of the Tribulation arrives, it is meant to be an indicator to Jewish believers to flee to the mountains. God will protect them if they flee to the mountains, but if they stay in Jerusalem they will be killed. There are certain mountain ranges they are instructed to flee to. How will Jewish believers know when and where to flee? Through knowledge of the Word of God.

Matthew 24:17-18:

Let him which is on the housetop not come down to take any thing out of his house:

Neither let him which is in the field return back to take his clothes.

The very day Antichrist walks into the temple and demands to be worshiped, some will be relaxing at home; others will be working in the fields, but all are commanded to run to the mountains as quickly as possible. They are not even to take time to gather clothing or to take anything from their homes. They are to run to the mountains as quickly as possible. Daniel 11:41 names the mountains they are to flee to.

Daniel 11:41:

He shall enter also into the glorious land, and many countries shall be overthrown: but these shall escape out of his hand, even Edom, and Moab, and the chief of the children of Ammon.

Jewish believers are to are to run to the mountain ranges of Edom, Moab, and Ammon. These mountain ranges surround the Dead Sea. These are the same mountain ranges where Baalam prophesied. They are the same mountain ranges of three heathen nations: Edom, Moab, and Ammon. God is going to turn cursing into blessing. The very mountains representing three nations that fought against Israel, God will turn to blessing for His people.

Matthew 24:19-20:

And woe unto them that are with child, and to them that give suck in those days!

But pray ye that your flight be not in the winter, neither on the Sabbath day:

Fleeing to the mountains will be difficult enough in itself, but being pregnant will be even more difficult. If it happens during the winter, the mountains will be more difficult to travel. If it happens on the Sabbath, it will also make it more difficult to flee, because all of the shops will be closed. There would be no place to buy provisions on the way to the mountains!

Matthew 24:21:

For then shall be great tribulation, such as was not since the beginning of the world to this time, no, nor ever shall be.

The second half of the Tribulation is called the Great Tribulation. It will be the worst time that has ever existed in history. The reason the second half will be worse than the first half of the Tribulation is because Satan will be cast out of heaven at that time. He will no longer be allowed to operate there. Satan is called the accuser of the brethren. Just as he walked into God's presence to accuse Job, he does the same thing with us today (Revelation 12:10, Romans 8:33). However, once he is finally removed from heaven, he will no longer have access. When he is thrown into the earth, he will realize his days are numbered and will unleash all of his fury. When Antichrist walks in to take over the throne, he wants all men to realize he,

Satan, is god and his man, Antichrist, will be worshiped. The minute Satan is cast from heaven, vials, wrath, woe, killings, slaughter, and great upheavals of nature will occur. Antichrist will demand all to worship him and demand all Jews be killed, especially Jewish Christians. Those who know the Word will flee to the mountains and be protected by God.

Matthew 24:22:

> *And except those days should be shortened, there should not flesh be saved: but for the elect's sake those days shall be shortened.*

The second half of the Tribulation is called the *Great* Tribulation and God will not allow it to go one day beyond three and a half years because of the believers in the earth. If Jesus did not return on the last day of the seven year Tribulation, there will be so much destructed in the earth Israel would no longer exist.

Matthew 24:23-26:

> *Then if any man shall say unto you, Lo, here is Christ, or there; believe it not.*

*For there shall arise false Christs, and false
prophets, and shall show great signs and wonders;
insomuch that, if it were possible, they shall deceive
the very elect.*

Behold, I have told you before.

*Wherefore if they shall say unto you, Behold, he is
in the desert; go not forth: behold, he is in the secret
chambers; believe it not.*

The only way Antichrist can kill Christians is to lure
them away from the mountains where they are protected
by God. The way he will deceive some to come down
from the mountains is by telling them Jesus has come
and is looking for them. He will say, "Jesus is looking for
you. Look, He is in your bedroom searching for you." I
would imagine they will have televisions and computers
in the mountains and Satan will probably project a false
Jesus searching through houses of believers. He may even
call them by name. Believers must know the Word so
they will not be lured. These verses say, "Don't believe
these things." There may be a few who will believe these
deceptions and as soon as they leave the mountain, they
will be killed because they will no longer be under the
protection of God. Satan will perform lying signs and
wonders to deceive believers, but if a believer has a choice

between a *supernatural sign* and wonder of the *Word of God*, they should always go with the Word of God. If signs and wonders are verified by the Word, they are from God. However, Satan can also perform signs and wonders and the standard of judgment must be the Word of God. The signs and wonders may tell these tribulational saints to come down from the mountains, but the Word says to stay. They must heed the Word or die.

The Second Advent

Matthew 24:27:

> *For as lightning cometh out of the east, and shineth even unto the west; so shall also the coming of the Son of man be.*

Jesus is going to come back as lightning from the east to the west. This is not the rapture of the church; this is the Second Coming of Jesus!

Matthew 24:28:

> *For wheresoever the carcase is, there will the eagles be gathered together.*

The Battle of Armageddon is the event that will draw Jesus back. The word for "eagles" is actually "vultures." This verse describes that battle as buzzards or vultures circling around a dead carcass. Israel will be at the Battle of Armageddon and will be as defenseless as a dead carcass. The dead carcass is Israel and the vultures circling are all the nations of the world coming against Israel. This battle is described in great detail in Joel, chapters two and three, and Zechariah, chapters ten through fourteen.

During the battle of Armageddon, half the city of Jerusalem will be taken and there will be many led into captivity. It will appear as a repeat of what happened in 70 A.D. when the Romans captured Jerusalem, but this battle will be different. In the middle of the battle, Jesus Christ will return to deliver the Jews, destroy the armies coming against Israel, and liberate the city of Jerusalem.

There are two comings of the Lord yet to occur: *the rapture of the church* and the *Second Advent.* At the Rapture, the church will be delivered from its curse; the nature of the flesh will be removed. At the Second Advent, nature will be delivered. What is the great hope of the church? The Rapture. What is the great hope of nature and the world? The Second Advent.

Romans 8:21:

Because the creation itself also shall be delivered from the bondage of corruption into the glorious liberty of the children of God.

When the church returns with the Lord Jesus Christ at the Second Coming, we will return with our resurrection bodies—no curse attached. The moment we return, nature will be released from its bondage of corruption into the glorious liberty of the children of God. When Jesus comes back with the church, nature will join the church in being free from the curse. Deuteronomy, the Psalms, and Jesus Himself all tell us nature will break forth into glorious liberty. The seas will clap their hands, the trees will clap their hands, the rocks will cry out and nature will break forth in singing.

Picture Jesus coming back from heaven riding on a white horse to fight the Battle of Armageddon and ten thousands of his saints coming with Him crying and singing, "King of kings and Lord of lords!" The moment Jesus breaks through the atmosphere, nature will be released from its bondage and there will be an antiphonal of both nature and the church singing forth "King of kings and Lord of lords!" What a glorious day that will be!

Romans 8:22-23:

For we know that the whole creation groaneth and travaileth in pain together until now.

And not only they, but ourselves also, which have the firstfruits of the Spirit, even we ourselves groan within ourselves, waiting for the adoption, to wit, the redemption of our body.

We are waiting for the Rapture. Nature is waiting for the Second Advent. At the Rapture, our curse is removed. At the Second Advent, nature's curse is removed. Both of us are waiting for the coming of the Lord.

These two verses of scripture say nature groans and travails. We also, groan and travail. Groaning and travailing are birth terms. With every earthquake, nature is groaning and travailing. With every famine and outbreak of pestilence, nature is groaning and travailing. With every war and rumor of war, nature is having a contraction. The same thing is true of the church. Every tribulation, trial, and trouble we go through causes us to groan and travail under the pressure of it. The earth is pregnant with the millennial reign, but the church is pregnant with our resurrection body. One day the church will give birth. On that day there will be no more travail, no more pressure. We will break forth into the glorious liberty of a child of

God! When that day comes, not only will our spirit be redeemed, not only will our soul be redeemed, our body will be redeemed! What a hope and a future we have!

Matthew 24:27 says Jesus will return from heaven as lightning from the east to the west. At the Second Advent, every eye will see Him. Every tribe will see Him. Every tongue will confess Him as Lord. Believers will see Him. Unbelievers will see Him. Kings will see Him and peasants will see Him. Every man, woman, and child on the earth will see Him because He will come back as lightning from the east to the west, and this lightning will not be like natural lightning. It will be the glory of God Matthew mentioned in chapter 17 when He stood with Moses and Elijah and *His face did shine as the sun and His raiment was as white as light.* Jesus will be clothed with the glory of God! In majesty He will return to rule and reign forever!

8

The Second Coming

The End of the Tribulation

During the time of the Tribulation, the church will be judged in heaven at the judgment seat of Christ. Also during that time, many multiplied millions of people will receive Jesus Christ as their Lord and Savior. At the end of the seven years of the Tribulation, the church will return with Jesus at His Second Coming. When Jesus returns, the earth will be filled with both believers and unbelievers. As previously mentioned, evangelism will go from zero to worldwide in that brief seven-year period. When Jesus returns, He will separate believers from unbelievers.

Matthew 3:11-12:

...he shall baptize you with the Holy Ghost, and with fire:

Whose fan is in his hand, and he will thoroughly purge his floor, and gather his wheat into the garner; but he will burn up the chaff with unquenchable fire.

In these verses, believers are called *"wheat"* and unbelievers are called *"chaff."* It is difficult to distinguish the difference between wheat and chaff. They look very similar to one another. Matthew 13 talks about the difficulty of distinguishing between the wheat and the tares. Both cases are a description of the believer and the unbeliever. In both cases the wheat is kept and the chaff or tares are burned up. Matthew 13 also compares believers and unbelievers to good fish and bad fish. The good fish are kept and the bad fish are thrown away. Matthew 25 gives the analogy of sheep (believers) and goats (unbelievers).

At the end of the Tribulation, the believers who were born again during the Tribulation will be separated from the unbelievers. Believers will go into the millennial reign of the Lord Jesus Christ and be rewarded. Unbelievers will go into Hell to wait for the great white throne judgment where they will be sentenced to the lake of fire forever. Many rewards will be given to believers on the earth at that time. They will have children. They will have natural bodies but longevity will be restored and the earth will return to a time very similar to the days of Noah when people lived for hundreds of years. The curse will be lifted from the earth. Life will be comparable to the Garden of Eden. Even though man will still have the nature of the flesh, the earth will be perfect. At the beginning of the millennium, only Christians will be on earth. There will be no Satan, no demons, and no unbelievers. Because the curse will have been lifted, hindrances will be removed. Jesus Christ will rule and reign. Hindrances to having children will be removed. Hindrances to wealth will be removed. Hindrances to businesses will be removed. The earth will proliferate with children and finances. Even with everything in a perfect state, some will reject the Lord during the millennium. At the end of the millennium those who reject Jesus will be rounded up by Satan for one last battle.

Matthew 24:29-30:

Immediately after the tribulation of those days shall the sun be darkened and the moon shall not give her light, and the stars shall fall from heaven [literally, they will be blotted out], *and the powers of the heavens shall be shaken:*

And then shall appear the sign of the Son of man in heaven: and then shall all the tribes of the earth mourn...

This does not happen at the Rapture. The sun will keep shining at the Rapture, the moon will keep shining at the Rapture, and the stars will keep shining. When Jesus returns at the Rapture, only Christians will see him and rise to meet Him in the air. Unbelievers will only see that one minute believers are here and the next they are gone. But at the Second Coming, every eye will see Him, both believers and unbelievers. The best way to describe what will happen at the Second Advent is it will be exactly opposite of the Rapture. Unbelievers will be removed from the earth and believers will remain.

Matthew 24:30-31:

... and they shall see the Son of man coming in the clouds of heaven with power and great glory.

And he shall send his angels with a great sound of a trumpet, and they shall gather together his elect from the four winds, from one end of heaven to the other.

His elect are believers. The elect will be gathered together for protection from the wrath of God which will be poured out on the earth. God's wrath will fall on all unbelievers and the angels will help protect believers from that day so they will be unharmed.

When Jesus returns to establish His kingdom, all unbelievers who were on earth at the end of the Tribulation will be sentenced to hell for a thousand years. Hell is merely a waiting place for the final place called "the lake of fire."

The Parable of the Fig Tree

Matthew 24:32:

Now learn a parable of the fig tree; When his branch is yet tender, and putteth forth leaves, ye know that summer is nigh:

Throughout the Word of God, Israel is seen as a fig tree. *"Summer"* is the Millennium. Buds come out in the spring and spring indicates summer is near. When Israel begins to bud and blossom, we know that the Millennium is very, very near. How near? Notice the verses that follow:

Matthew 24:33-35:

So likewise ye, when ye shall see all these things, know that it is near, even at the doors.

Verily I say unto you, This generation shall not pass, till all these things be fulfilled.

Heaven and earth shall pass away, but my words shall not pass away.

The generation that will not pass is the generation that sees the fig tree begin to bud. The generation that will not

179

pass is the generation that sees all of the things previously mentioned come to pass; the Tribulation, the sun, moon, and stars being darkened, Jesus coming back as lightning from the east to the west, angels protecting people from the wrath of God. The generation that sees the fig tree blossom and bud, *that* generation will not pass away until all these things come to pass. Although these verses are referring to a specific group of people, it is also referring to a specific length of time. There is much debate about what entails a generation. Some say forty years, others sixty. Somewhere in the span of forty to sixty years is considered a generation.

Again, verse 32 tells us when Israel (the fig tree) brings forth buds, the Millennium is very near. In 1948, Israel became a nation and in 1966, they regained the city of Jerusalem. Over the years men have tried to speculate and calculate when the rapture of the church will occur based on these significant dates in Israel, but every time they have guessed, they have been wrong. I personally believe we are the generation that will see His return. Sometime in our general lifetime, I believe we will be Raptured and seven years later we will return with the Lord at the Second Advent.

Every verse of scripture has one interpretation and many applications. In the portion of scripture following, there are many applications, but we will study the interpretation. To study interpretation, the verses must be kept in context.

Again, Matthew 24 and 25 are in chronological order and that is how we will examine them.

Matthew 24:36:

> *But of that day and hour knoweth no man, no, not the angels of heaven, but my Father only.*

Keeping this event in context, the *"day"* being referred to is the Second Advent. This verse says the Father alone, knows when that day will occur.

As in the Days of Noah

Matthew 24:37:

> *But as the days of Noe* (Noah) *were, so shall also the coming of the Son of man be.*

This verse is still referring to the Second Advent. Again, the verses in this section of scripture are chronological. Immediately following the Tribulation, Jesus will come back as lightning from the east to the west. Angels will gather together His elect to protect them from the wrath of God to come, unbelievers will be removed from the earth, and believers will enter into the millennial reign of Jesus Christ.

181

Jude 14:

And Enoch also, the seventh from Adam, prophesied of these...

"These" are false prophets spoken of in the previous verses. The same type of false prophets that are seen rising up in our day will appear throughout the Tribulation. In fact, Jesus warned that more false prophets will arise during the Tribulation than the world has ever seen.

... saying, Behold, the Lord cometh with ten thousands of his saints,

Jude 15:

To execute judgment upon all, and to convince all that are ungodly among them of all their ungodly deeds which they have ungodly committed, and of all their hard speeches which ungodly sinners have spoken against him.

Enoch prophesied and said he saw the Lord coming with ten thousands of his saints to execute judgment on the earth against all sinners, especially the false prophets who led others astray. It is interesting that Enoch had a vision of the Second Advent of the Lord. Genesis tells us

Enoch did not walk with God until he had a son named Methuselah. Apparently, he had not lived a godly life prior to Methuselah's birth. What caused Enoch to decide to live a godly life? The answer is found in the name "Methuselah." Methuselah means, "when he dies, it shall fall." What an odd name. The most significant fact about Methuselah is he lived longer than any person has ever lived on earth. He lived 969 years! If you calculate years according to the ages listed throughout Genesis, chapter 5, you will discover Methuselah died the same year the flood came. God instructed Enoch to name his son Methuselah, and through that name Enoch knew the flood was coming. Before the flood came, Enoch was raptured!

At the time of the flood, the ungodly were removed and the godly were left on the earth. Again, Matthew 24:37 says, *"As the days of Noah were, so shall also the coming of the Son of man be."* What is the parallel between the events of Noah's day and the Second Coming of Jesus Christ? The flood of Noah ended one dispensation and began another. When Noah and his family entered the ark, it was one dispensation. When they finally left the ark, another dispensation had begun. When Noah and his family walked out of the ark and onto the dry ground, there was not one sinner left. All had died in the flood. For a short time, the entire earth was populated with only believers.

Noah preached to the people to repent. His message was "Repent! Destruction is coming! If you'll repent, you'll go through the destruction, come out on the other side, and be able to repopulate the earth. The best part of it is, when the destruction has ended, we can start over again and only believers will be on the earth!" The difference is, in Noah's day God judged the earth by water, but the next judgment will be by fire.

Matthew 24:38:

For as in the days that were before the flood they were eating and drinking, marrying and giving in marriage, until the day that Noe (Noah) entered into the ark,

Those who were eating, drinking, marrying, and giving in marriage were unbelievers. None of these activities are sin. These inhabitants of the Tribulation were trying to live normal lives, ignore the gospel and ignore the circumstances surrounding them. Sinners continued to ignore the building of the ark and the preaching and prophecies of Noah. When the day finally came for Noah and his family to enter the ark, the rain began to fall, they pulled the door shut, and the sinners began pounding on the door to enter. But once the door shut, it was too late.

In the same way, during the Tribulation people will be eating, drinking, marrying and giving in marriage. Again, there is nothing wrong with these things but people will ignore the gospel being preached and the signs and circumstances surrounding their lives. While wrath is being poured out on the earth—floods, a scorching sun, multitudes dying, the Antichrist ruling and putting his mark on hands or foreheads—the unbelievers will continue attempting to live normal lives. When Jesus Christ does return, no opportunities will remain for them to receive Him as Lord and Savior.

Matthew 24:39:

> *And knew not until the flood came, and took them all away; so shall also the coming of the Son of man be.*

The *"them"* that were taken away when the flood came were not believers. The unbelievers were taken away.

Matthew 24:40:

> *Then shall two be in the field; the one shall be taken, and the other left.*

At the Second Advent, just as in the days of Noah, the one taken will be the unbeliever and the one left will be the believer.

Matthew 24:41:

Two women shall be grinding at the mill; the one shall be taken, and the other left.

Again, the one who is taken is the unbeliever and the one who is left is the believer.

Matthew 24:42-44:

Watch therefore: for ye know not what hour your Lord doth come.

But know this, that if the goodman of the house had known in what watch the thief would come, he would have watched, and would not have suffered his house to be broken up.

Therefore be ye also ready: for in such an hour as ye think not the Son of man cometh.

These verses are simply warning that Jesus will return and although the specific day and hour will not be known, the general time period will be known. Right up until that time, many will say, "Well, maybe Jesus is coming, but I really don't need to be saved right now. I think I'll just put it off." Even after the rapture of the Church, people will still have seven more years to be saved. During the Tribulation, some of the parables indicate that at least half of the population will receive Jesus Christ as their Savior.

Three Parables About the Second Coming

At the end of Matthew 24 and continuing into Matthew 25, Jesus will share three parables. Jesus continues with His thought. He has not changed the subject. In the context and chronology of these passages, all three parables will be referring to the Second Coming of Jesus Christ. The first parable deals with servants, the second with virgins, and the third with stewards. In each case, some will be good and the others will be bad. Those who are good are believers and those who are bad are unbelievers. Why will both the good and the bad be called by the same name? Both good and bad will be called *servants*. Both good and bad will be called *virgins*. Both good and bad will be called *stewards*. Just as it is difficult to distinguish between a good and bad fish, or wheat and tares, or sheep and goats, so it will be difficult to distinguish believers from unbelievers until they are closely examined.

During the Tribulation, the earth will be filled with a central religion. Satan has created religion to imitate Christianity. Muslims, like Christians, tell the story of Abraham, but they teach that the chosen son was Ishmael. They also teach their prophet, Mohammad, stood in Jerusalem on a mountain and was resurrected into heaven. Others may compare the similarities of their religion to Christianity, but Christianity is real other religions are false.

Religious people look and talk like Christians. They may even do more good works than Christians do, but how a person looks or acts is not the issue. The issue is whether or not a person has accepted Jesus and believed on Him for salvation. The first parable deals with the good and evil servant.

Parable of the Good Servant and Evil Servant

Matthew 24:45-47:

Who then is a faithful and wise servant, whom his lord hath made ruler over his household, to give them meat in due season?

Blessed is that servant, whom his lord when he cometh shall find so doing.

Verily I say unto you, That he shall make him ruler over all his goods.

At the Second Advent, the believer will not only be allowed to go into the Millennium, He will also be rewarded. There will be rewards for those who come through the Tribulation and endure to the end.

Matthew 24:48-49:

But and if that evil servant shall say in his heart, My lord delayeth his coming;

And shall begin to smite his fellowservants, and to eat and drink with the drunken;

Again, the people were eating and drinking in Noah's day and many probably said, *"We'll just wait a little longer before we accept the Lord."*

Matthew 24:50-51:

The lord of that servant shall come in a day when he looketh not for him, and in an hour that he is not aware of,

And shall cut him asunder, and appoint him his portion with the hypocrites: there shall be weeping and gnashing of teeth.

On the day the Lord returns, there will be good servants and bad servants; wise servants and unwise servants. The wise servant will say, "I love my Lord and have accepted Him." This servant will do good things during the Tribulation. He will go into the Millennium and receive rewards of rulership with Jesus on earth. The wicked servant will say, "My Lord delays His coming." This servant will be removed from earth and find his portion in hell with the hypocrites where there is weeping and gnashing of teeth.

The second parable begins in Matthew, chapter 25. This is a poor place to have a chapter division. The first word of this chapter is *"Then"* indicating that there is a continuation of thought. *"Then"* is a reference to the Second Advent. Just as in the days of Noah, unbelievers will be removed from the earth and believers will be left. There will be two in a field; one will be taken, the other left. The one taken will be the unbeliever. There will be two grinding; one will be taken, and the other left. Again, the one taken will be the unbeliever and the one remaining will be the believer.

Parable of the Ten Virgins

Matthew 25:1-2:

Then shall the kingdom of heaven be likened unto ten virgins, which took their lamps, and went forth to meet the bridegroom.

And five of them were wise, and five were foolish.

Notice, all of the virgins know the bridegroom is coming and go to meet him, but five of the virgins will be wise and five will be foolish. They know the Lord is coming but put off the decision to put their trust in Him. The five wise virgins are believers and the unwise are unbelievers.

Matthew 25:3-4:

They that were foolish took their lamps, and took no oil with them:

But the wise took oil in their vessels with their lamps.

What is the difference between the wise and the foolish virgins? Both look and act like Christians, but five have oil and five do not. In other words, five are born again and five are not. Both said, "Lord, Lord" but the unwise virgins never accepted Jesus as their Lord and Savior. We have many in our churches today who look and act like they are born again. They may volunteer, shout "Amen" during a sermon and say, "Praise the Lord!" They know what to do to be saved, but never accept Jesus as their Savior. I believe there are people sitting in congregations every Sunday who keep saying, "I know I should get saved, but I think I'll just wait." But if you are a sinner, there is no guarantee of tomorrow. If these people do not accept Jesus before the Rapture, they will have just seven more years to accept Him.

During the Tribulation there will be those waiting for the return of the bridegroom. Some will have accepted Him as Lord and Savior and others will keep putting it off, just as many do today. The virgins do not represent the bride, they represent friends of the bride, those in the wedding party waiting for the bridegroom to return.

In the day in which this parable was written, wedding customs were different than today. The traditional ceremonies of our day began five or six hundred years ago and were instituted by the Catholic Church. In biblical times, marriage was an agreement. Basically, it was a business transaction between the father of the bride and the groom. This is where the dowry came into play. The father and the groom would discuss the terms of the agreement until a settlement was made and a wedding date determined.

Once the wedding date was determined, plans were made for the wedding party. The wedding party did not occur until after the marriage. All of the friends of the bride and all of the friends of the groom were invited to a celebration, which took place at the home of the groom. Until the groom came for the bride, she would be preparing herself for the wedding day. When the day finally arrived, the groom went to the home of the bride. Her father would take her by the hand, lead her to the groom and at this point they were legally married. Really, in the ancient world marriage was not a ceremony. Marriage was a contract sealed by sex. After the father gave the bride to the groom, the groom would take her to his home, and lead her into the bedchamber. The moment the bride and groom entered the house, the wedding party followed and they began to celebrate the marriage. While the celebration was taking place, the bride and groom would have sexual relations to consummate the marriage. In the ancient world, these parties could last up to a month. From time to time, the bride and groom would join the wedding party to eat and drink and then return to the bedchamber.

Here is the analogy. Jesus Christ fell in love with us and asked the Father if we could be His bride. The Father said, "Yes. The day is coming." Just as the bride was preparing for the groom, for the seven years of the Tribulation, the

Church will be prepared for the Bridegroom. This is the purpose of the Judgment Seat of Christ. The marriage supper of the Lamb will not occur in heaven; it will occur on earth. Jesus is going to return from heaven, back to earth, His house. The Bible says, *"The earth is the Lord's and the fullness thereof"* (Psalm 24:1). During the Tribulation, Jesus will win many friends. The friends will be the virgins with oil. Those who are saved and indwelt by the Holy Spirit. Jesus will see those whose lamps are burning—those who have accepted Him. They are His friends who will be invited to the marriage supper of the Lamb.

Matthew 25:5-6:

While the bridegroom tarried, they all slumbered and slept.

And at midnight there was a cry made, Behold, the bridegroom cometh; go ye out to meet him.

Those going out to meet the bridegroom are not the bride, these are friends of the bride and groom who have been waiting for the return of the bridegroom with his bride.

Matthew 25:7-9:

Then all those virgins arose, and trimmed (lit) *their lamps.*

And the foolish said unto the wise, Give us of your oil; for our lamps are gone out.

But the wise answered, saying, Not so; lest there be not enough for us and you: but go ye rather to them that sell, and buy for yourselves.

The wise virgins tell the unwise, "There are people preaching for you to get born again. All you need to do is accept salvation. We cannot give you our salvation. You have to accept Jesus as your own personal Savior. The decision is yours."

Matthew 25:10:

And while they went to buy, the bridegroom came; and they that were ready went in with him to the marriage: and the door was shut.

Notice, the door was shut, just as it was in Noah's day. The unwise virgins delayed accepting Jesus as their Lord and Savior until there no longer remained an opportunity to receive Him. They waited until it was too late.

Matthew 25:11-13:

> *Afterward came also the other virgins, saying, Lord, Lord, open to us.*

> *But he answered and said, Verily I say unto you, I know you not.*

> *Watch therefore, for ye know neither the day nor the hour wherein the Son of man cometh.*

Once the door was shut, the five foolish virgins could no longer enter. In the third parable, the same theme is repeated: Believers and unbelievers.

Parable of the Talents

Matthew 25:14-15:

> *For the kingdom of heaven is as a man traveling into a far country, who called his own servants, and delivered unto them his goods.*

And unto one he gave five talents, to another two, and to another one; to every man according to his several ability; and straightway took his journey.

The talents given to each servant represent the receiving and sharing of the gospel. Each servant was given talents according to his ability. Each person is unique and individual. The individual given five talents who produced five additional talents will not be more greatly rewarded than the servant given two talents who produced an additional two talents. God gives to each man what He knows that individual can handle.

Matthew 25:16-18:

Then he that had received the five talents went and traded with the same, and made them other five talents.

And likewise he that had received two, he also gained other two.

But he that had received one went and digged in the earth, and hid his lord's money.

The servant who was given one talent was an unbeliever. This individual heard the gospel but did not receive it. Instead, he buried it. The other two servants heard and received the gospel. Then they shared the gospel with others.

Matthew 25:19:

After a long time the lord of those servants cometh, and reckoneth with them.

The Lord returning is not a reference to the Rapture; it is a reference to the Second Coming. Some will go through the Tribulation, receive Jesus as their Lord and Savior and win souls, and some will not.

Matthew 25:20-21:

And so he that had received five talents came and brought other five talents, saying, Lord, thou delivered unto me five talents: behold, I have gained beside them five talents more.

His lord said unto him, Well done, thou good and faithful servant: thou hast been faithful over a few things, I will make thee ruler over many things: enter thou into the joy of they lord.

The "joy of the lord" is a reference to the millennial reign. "Ruler over many things" refers to rewards given during the millennial reign of Jesus Christ.

Matthew 25:22-23:

> *He also that had received two talents came and said, Lord, thou delivered unto me two talents: behold, I have gained two other talents beside them.*
>
> *His lord said unto him, Well done, good and faithful servant; thou hast been faithful over a few things, I will make thee ruler over many things: enter thou into the joy of thy lord.*

Because of what the servant has done with the talents he has been given, the Lord will give him rulership during His millennial reign.

Matthew 25:24-25:

> *Then he which had received the one talent came and said, Lord, I knew thee that thou art an hard man, reaping where thou hast not sown, and gathering where thou hast not strawed:*

And I was afraid, and went and hid thy talent in the earth: lo, there thou hast that is thine.

Notice, this servant tried to return the talent. The other two servants had received the talents, invested them, and received more. However, this servant took the talent and immediately buried it in the ground. In other words, he heard the gospel and rejected it. When the Lord returned the servant said, "I've heard rumors about You. I heard You are hard and harsh. I heard You are mean and reap where You haven't sown—that You harvest where You have never planted. This is why I didn't receive You!" Even today we hear unbelievers say, "Why would I want to serve a God Who causes wars? Why would I want to serve a God Who causes people to starve in the streets?" They are given the truth about His goodness, His character, His desire for them to be saved, but they refuse to accept Jesus as their Lord and Savior.

Matthew 25:26-27:

His lord answered and said unto him, Thou wicked and slothful servant, thou knewest that I reap where I sowed not, and gather where I have not strawed:

Thou oughtest therefore to have put my money to the exchangers (in a bank), *and then at my coming I should have received mine own with usury.*

He said to the servant, "The least you could have done is receive salvation for yourself, but you didn't even do that. You dug a hole in the ground and buried your talent and then tried to give it back to Me!"

Matthew 25:28-30:

Take therefore the talent from him, and give it unto him which hath ten talents.

For unto every one that hath shall be given, and he shall have abundance: but from him that hath not shall be taken away even that which he hath.

And cast ye the unprofitable servant into outer darkness: there shall be weeping and gnashing of teeth.

Notice, in the first parable we had one good and one evil servant. In the parable of the ten virgins there were five wise and five foolish virgins. In each case, half were wise (believers) and half were unwise (unbelievers). In the third parable, two of the three servants accepted Jesus as their

Lord and Savior. The first two parables seem to indicate at least half of all people alive during the Tribulation will come to know Jesus as their Lord and Savior and the third parable indicates two-thirds will receive Him as their Savior!

Throughout chapters 24 and 25 of Matthew, Jesus has been teaching in parables. A parable is simply a story about the truth, using natural analogies to teach a truth. In the next verse, Jesus shifts from speaking in parables to speaking of events as they will actually occur.

9

The Millennial Reign of the Lord Jesus Christ

A Perfect Environment

During the Millennium, the atmosphere of the earth will be perfect. Satan and the demons will be removed and it will begin with believers only. Everything on earth will be perfect because there will be no opposition. The weather will be perfect, business will be perfect, longevity will be restored, children will never be harmed, and the earth will be in peace. Some wonder why the Millennium is even necessary. They wonder, "Why not just go to heaven and live forever there?"

Personally, I believe Jesus Christ will use the thousand years of the Millennium to disprove one of man's greatest and most long-lived theories about mankind. The theory is *if man had a perfect environment in which to live, all of man's problems would be solved.* A perfect environment is not the answer; regeneration is the solution. For years man has said, "If we can just remove man out of the ghetto, give him an education, find him a job, everything will work out fine." Man's problem is not what is outside him, it is what is in his heart. And only regeneration can change his heart.

God is going to give man a thousand years of a perfect environment. During that thousand years, people will be born who will refuse to accept Jesus Christ. At the end of the Millennium, the Bible says Satan will be released for "a season" and an army of unbelievers will join him in one last rebellion against God.

Just imagine the world being perfect in every way with Jesus ruling and reigning. No Satan. No demons. Perfect in every respect and yet, some born during the Millennium will not receive Jesus as their Savior. The Millennium will disprove man's theory that a perfect environment will cause man to live perfectly before God.

The Parable of the Sheep and Goats

Matthew 25 continues describing the events occurring at the second coming of Jesus Christ.

Matthew 25:31:

When the Son of man shall come in his glory, and all the holy angels with him, then shall he sit upon the throne of his glory:

This verse is describing what will occur following Armageddon at the Second Advent. When destruction comes, believers will remain and all unbelievers will be removed from the earth.

Matthew 25:32:

And before him shall be gathered all nations: and he shall separate them one from another, as a shepherd divideth his sheep from the goats:

Again, the sheep will be the righteous; the goats will be the unrighteous. The sheep will be the virgins with oil; the goats will be the virgins without oil. The sheep will be the wise servants; the goats will be the servants that are wicked. The sheep will be the wise stewards; the goats will be the unwise stewards.

Matthew 25:33-34:

And he shall set the sheep on his right hand, but the goats on the left.

Then (the Second Advent) *shall the King say unto all those on his right hand, Come, you blessed of my Father, inherit the kingdom prepared for you from the foundation of the world.*

The *"kingdom"* is the millennial reign that has been predicted and prophesied throughout the Old and New Testaments, prepared from the foundation of the world.

Matthew 25:35-41:

For I was an hungered, and ye gave me meat: I was thirsty, and ye gave me drink: I was a stranger, and ye took me in:

Naked, and ye clothed me: I was sick, and ye visited me: I was in prison, and ye came unto me.

Then (the Second Advent) *shall the righteous answer him, saying, Lord, when saw we thee an hungered, and fed thee? or thirsty, and gave thee drink?*

When saw we thee a stranger, and took thee in? or naked, and clothed thee?

Or when saw we thee sick, or in prison, and came unto thee?

And the King shall answer and say unto them, Verily I say unto you, Inasmuch as ye have done it unto one of the least of these my brethren, ye have done it unto me.

*Then shall he say also unto them on the left hand,
Depart from me, ye cursed, into everlasting fire,
prepared for the devil and his angels:*

Notice, in these verses both the righteous and the
unrighteous are mentioned. The righteous are believers
and the unrighteous are unbelievers. Notice, too, hell was
never prepared for people. It was originally intended for
Satan, the fallen angels, and demons. However, since there
are some people who choose to reject Jesus and follow
Satan, they will be banished to the same place Satan is
banished for eternity. Those who accept Jesus and follow
God will spend eternity in heaven with Him.

Matthew 25:42-46:

*For I was hungered, and ye gave me not meat; I was
thirsty, and ye gave me not drink;*

*I was a stranger, and ye took me not in: naked, and
ye clothed me not: sick, and in prison, and ye visited
me not.*

*Then shall they also answer him, saying, Lord, when
saw we thee an hungered, or athirst, or a stranger, or*

*naked, or sick, or in prison, and did not minister unto
thee?*

*Then shall he answer them, saying, Verily I say unto
you, Inasmuch as ye did it not to one of the least of
these, ye did it not to me.*

*And these shall go away into everlasting punishment:
but the righteous into life eternal.*

"Everlasting punishment" is a reference to hell and
"life eternal" is a reference to the millennial reign of
the Lord Jesus Christ. The book of Matthew has several
parallel verses.

Matthew 3:11:

*I indeed baptize you with water unto repentance:
but he that cometh after me is mightier than I, whose
shoes I am not worthy to bear: he shall baptize you
with the Holy Ghost, and with fire:*

John the Baptist was addressing believers and
unbelievers. He was saying, "There is One coming after
me who is mightier than me. I'm not even worthy to
latch His shoes. When He comes He will baptize you—
believers—with the Holy Ghost. And He will baptize

you—unbelievers, Pharisees, Sadducees, religious scribes—with fire." The next verse further explains.

Matthew 3:12:

Whose fan is in his hand, and he will thoroughly purge his floor, and gather his wheat into the garner; but he will burn up the chaff with unquenchable fire.

The "floor" is the earth. One day He will thoroughly purge it. The "wheat" (believers) will be gathered into the garner—will go into millennial reign of the Lord Jesus Christ. But the "chaff" (unbelievers) will be burned up with unquenchable fire.

Other parallels we have already examined, are found throughout the thirteenth chapter of Matthew. There are seven parables dealing with the Church, the Tribulation, and the beginning of the Millennium. Again, there are good fish and bad fish, sheep and goats, wheat and chaff, all representing the fact that at the Second Advent, all unbelievers will be removed from the earth and all believers will remain.

The Wheat and the Chaff

John the Baptist pointed out the wheat will be gathered into the garner and the chaff will be burned with unquenchable fire. To understand what John the Baptist is saying, it helps to understand how the wheat and chaff were separated in his day. During harvest time, the harvesters would gather both wheat and chaff from the fields. They would not try to separate them at that time. The wheat and chaff that had been gathered would be sent to women who did nothing but separate them from one another. Usually these women would either stand at the mouth of a cave or on a high hill where the wind would blow. They would scoop the grain with large round-shaped grain shovels and throw it into the air. Wheat weighs more than chaff, so each time the women would throw the mixture in the air, the wheat would fall back down and the chaff would be blown away by the wind. They would repeat this process over and over until all that remained was the wheat.

Notice, it is not the believer's responsibility to separate the wheat from the chaff; it is Jesus' responsibility. Our responsibility is to preach the gospel. So many Christians want to demonstrate and march against the causes of the unbeliever, but our responsibility is not to root out all of the evil through demonstrations. Our responsibility is to preach the gospel of Jesus Christ. We are to lay hands on the sick and see them recover. We are to cast out demons. We are to lead people to the Lord and pray for them to be filled with the Holy Spirit. When Jesus returns He will gather all of the wheat and chaff before Him—the good fish and the bad fish, the sheep and the goats, the wise and unwise virgins, the good and the wicked servants—He will gather all believers and unbelievers together, "throw" them into judgment and the wheat will remain. The believers will enter into the millennial reign of the Lord Jesus Christ. The chaff will be blown away. The unbelievers will be banished and burned with an unquenchable fire.

One Thousand Years of Peace

When Jesus returns and separates believers from unbelievers, the Millennium will begin. The Millennium will be one thousand years of peace. Ephesians 1:10 calls it *"...the dispensation of the fullness of times."* Notice, *"the dispensation"* (singular) *"of the fullness of times"* (plural). All times and dispensations ever in existance will be wrapped up in that one millennial dispensation. Some dispensations were Jewish, some were Gentile; but this final dispensation will be both Jewish and Gentile together. Both Jewish and Gentile believers will live in harmony together under the rulership of Jesus Christ. This will last for a thousand years.

All who come through the Tribulation will still have natural bodies. There will be great abundance in every way. Many babies will be born and there will be very little death. Death will occur during this time because capital punishment will exist. The Bible says Jesus will rule with a rod of iron (Revelation 19:15) during that time because lievers who rise up against His kingdom. ~~Many~~ ievers will at least obey the law, proliferate, and will not revolt against Jesus until the very end of the Millennium when Satan gathers them all together to rebel against Jesus Christ. When Satan is released for the last time, it will prove to the world that Satan has not and will not change. Some believe that Satan will one day be saved, but this is wrong thinking. He will never change. Satan will be cast into everlasting punishment. At the end of the Millennium, all unbelievers will stand before Jesus in heaven at the Great White Throne Judgment and those names not found written in the book of life are cast into the lake of fire for eternity.

At the end of the Millennium, all believers and unbelievers will receive resurrection bodies. These bodies will exist forever and forever. Believers will live with Jesus in these bodies for eternity, while unbelievers will be eternally in the lake of fire with Satan, the fallen angels, and demons.

A New Heaven and New Earth

After all of these things occur, Jesus will completely destroy the earth and the atmosphere around the earth. He will create a brand new heaven (the atmosphere around the earth) and earth. Why will he create a new heaven and earth? Because the current heaven and earth have been polluted by Satan. Satan is called the prince of the power of the air (Ephesians 2:2). The air is referring to the atmosphere around us. Jesus will destroy all of this and replace it with a brand new heaven and earth. The new earth is described in the last two chapters of Revelation, and will be completely different than the earth we now know.

The new earth will have no oceans. It will operate by completely different scientific principles. Oceans are currently necessary for rains to water the earth. The water evaporates off the oceans, forms clouds, the winds blow them over the earth, and the rains fall causing vegetation to grow. The excess waters flow back to the oceans and the process repeats itself again. Without oceans, the earth would not survive. With the new earth, a brand new principle will be set in motion. There will be no oceans. Neither will the earth be lit up by the sun or moon. Heaven, where God lives, will come and rest over the new earth and remain there forever. The earth will be lit by the glory of God. Heaven will light up the earth! Because the glory of God will be the light of the new earth, it will be different than the light we know. The glory of God comes from every direction. Anyone who works with lighting understands that to get rid of shadows, light must come from every direction. Heaven will light up the earth equally and there will be no shadows. There will not be a dark side to the earth. The Bible says in God there is no shadow of turning (James 1:17).

During that time, we will have access to both heaven and earth. We will also be able to go anywhere in the universe! Many people wonder why God made such a vast universe; He made it for us! When we have our resurrection bodies, we will be able to go anywhere in the universe.

God is light; that is one of His attributes. I believe God travels at a speed greater than the speed of light. I personally believe if man could exceed the speed of light, he would enter into God's dimension. Going beyond the speed of light is the separation of the natural world and spiritual world. I am thankful that angels travel more quickly than the speed of light because if I had troubled and called for help, if angels only traveled the speed of light, it would take them millions years to get to me! I do not believe angels travel at the speed of light; I believe they travel at the speed of thought.

Distance determines time. If a car travels sixty miles an hour, it will go one mile in a minute and sixty miles in an hour. The distance determines the time. But if you travel the speed of thought, you could travel one mile or sixty miles in the same amount of time! You would just think it and be there. In our resurrection bodies we will travel the speed of thought.

Positionally, man is above the angels but by creation we are below them. Angels are a superior creation, but that superior creation is just under us positionally. The moment we accept Jesus, angels become servants to those who are heirs of salvation. One day by creation we will be superior to angels. We will have resurrection bodies and travel wherever we want. The reason we will be superior to angels is because we will be redeemed, spirit, soul, and body, and the angels are not redeemed.

People often ask, "Won't we get bored in eternity?" I believe the universe alone is so infinite, every visible planet, sun, star, and moon we will have opportunity to explore in eternity. What has been discovered in the universe is incredible, but I believe we are only seeing a very small section of the universe. We are only seeing what is in our own backyard. We have yet to see all the vastness of it. One day we will be able to travel any place we desire. Our resurrection bodies will be able to exist in outer space or on any planet of the universe! Eye has not seen, nor ear heard, all that God has prepared for those who love Him (I Corinthians 2:9)!

10

Questions and Answers

1. **When Jesus was in hell for three days and three nights, did he fight with Satan?**

I don't believe Jesus fought with Satan during the time He was in hell. Satan opposed the resurrection of Jesus and I believe it was during His ascension that Jesus fought and defeated Satan.

2. **Where did Jesus' spirit go when He died?**

I believe Jesus' spirit went into hell, into Satan's domain. Romans 10:6-7 says, *"...Say not in thine heart, Who shall ascend into heaven? (that is, to bring Christ down from above:) Or, Who shall descend into the deep? (that is, to bring up Christ again from the dead.)"* The word "deep" is the Greek word "buthos" and means "abyss." The word "abyss" is used in Greek mythology, but in the New Testament, it is where the unbelievers go and where Satan will be bound for a thousand years. It is also where the fallen angels have been bound and will be released for a season during the Tribulation. The abyss is a place of torment, a place of chains, and after Satan is there for a thousand years, he will be cast into the lake of fire for eternity.

3. **In 1 Corinthians 15:52 when it says, *"...and the dead shall be raised incorruptible"* is this referring to the dead that are in Christ?**

The answer is yes. This is referring to believers who have died before us. There is a generation that will not see death but will be changed. This does not refer to Old Testament saints. Their resurrection will occur later.

4. **If you are out of fellowship when the rapture comes, will you still go to heaven?**

The answer is yes. God will not leave any part of His body here to be judged on the earth. All judgment occurs in heaven at the judgment seat of Christ. The Bible says we will be judged for our deeds, whether good or bad.

5. **What is the significance of being an ambassador for Christ?**

Second Corinthians 5:20 says we are ambassadors for Christ. An ambassador is a citizen of one country but is sent to another country to represent his home country. A Christian is not a citizen of this world; we are citizens of heaven. The moment we are saved, our citizenship changes from this world to heaven. We are in this world—a foreign country—representing heaven. An ambassador is sustained by the country from which he comes. God supplies all our needs according to His riches in glory by Christ Jesus. We should never fear the economy of this world because we are not supplied by the economy of this world. We are supplied by our home country. An ambassador lives by the laws of his home country, not the laws of the country in which he is living. If the laws of the country he is in violate the laws of the country he is from, he can claim diplomatic immunity. Satan says, "You have to be sick." But the believer says, "No, no. The rules of the country I'm from says, 'With the stripes of Jesus I am healed.'" We can claim diplomatic immunity from sickness and poverty. Also, when one country declares war on another, the first action taken is to remove all the ambassadors. You do not bomb your ambassadors with the enemy. You remove them and deal with them in their home country. The rapture is God bringing His ambassadors home. He will deal with them at the judgment seat of Christ. The Bible says they will be rewarded for the deeds done, whether good or bad. Some will receive many rewards and some will receive few (1 Corinthians 3:10-15). The good rewards are gold, silver, and precious stones. The bad are wood, hay, and stubble. Fire will descend and burn all that can be burned and we will be rewarded for what remains. The rapture of the Church is God bringing the whole family together to deal with us all at one time.

6.   If I am 80 years old when I die, will I look 80 years old in heaven?

Most scholars agree that Jesus died at the age of 33, and in heaven we will appear as we did when we were 33 years old on earth. But the other interesting thing is we will all recognize one another. When Peter, James, and John were on the mountain with Jesus at the transfiguration, they saw Moses and Elijah and knew exactly who they were, though they had never seen them before.

7.   Prior to receiving our resurrection body, what part of us goes to heaven when we die?

The real you goes to heaven. Your body is like a glove. When your hand is in the glove it has life. When the glove is removed, it has no life in itself but the hand still has life. When we die, the physical body no longer has life, but the real you (your spirit and soul) goes to be with the Lord. One day you will receive your resurrection body, which will be the completion of your redemption.

8. When a baby or child dies, will they be adults when they get to heaven?

I believe when children die, they will grow up and be taught in heaven. I do not have scripture to support that but have heard many people who have died and come back say that teaching goes on for children in heaven. It seems there would have to be teaching. A person would not want to be eternally an infant or child. And if you're pregnant when the rapture occurs, apparently somewhere between here and there the child will be born and will grow up in heaven.

9. What does the Bible say about cremation?

The Bible says absolutely nothing specifically about cremation. There is one recorded case of cremation in the Bible and the Bible did not say it was wrong. When Saul and Jonathan fell on their swords and killed themselves, they were cremated. If you really think about it, if cremation is unacceptable, what does that mean for Christians who have died in fires. Would that mean they would not be resurrected? The answer is no. Cremation is a personal decision.

10. Will we still have a spirit, soul, and body in eternity?

Yes, but the body will be radically different. We will have a resurrection body.

11. Does suicide separate a person from God?

No. Suicide does not separate a person from God. Saul is a perfect example of this. He committed suicide and was cremated. The day before he died, he went to a witch. The witch called up Samuel. People have debated back and forth, "Was that really Samuel or not?" I personally believe it was Samuel because Samuel said, "Why have you brought me up from a place of quiet?"

Next, the witch of Endor fell over backwards against the wall. She had never seen the real thing happen before. She was in shock! She had conjured up demons before, but she had never seen a real spirit come up. God allowed it to happen and Samuel said, "Why have you disquieted me?"

Saul asked, "Should I go to war or not?" And Samuel said, "Yes, go to war. You and your sons will be with me tomorrow." Saul and his sons committed suicide. There are many families still grieving because someone committed suicide. I believe if a Christian commits suicide, they have made a very wrong choice. However, they will be in heaven even though their arrival to heaven is premature. They will suffer lack of rewards, but they themselves will be saved.

12. Will teaching continue in heaven?

Yes, I believe we will still receiving teaching in heaven. The good news is we will only need to hear it one time! I believe in eternity we will never stop learning. I believe knowledge is as infinite as eternity and we won't forget anything we learn!

13. We will be in heaven for eternity?

The Bible doesn't say we will be in heaven forever; it says we will be with the Lord forever. We will be with Him in heaven for seven years. He will rule on earth for a thousand years. When there is a new heaven and earth, He will rule from heaven and from Jerusalem. The point is we will be with the Lord forever.

14. What happens to animals when they die?

Because animals do not have a spirit, animals do not go to heaven. This is a very controversial issue in my home. If you ask my wife, she'll give you an entirely different answer.

15. Will we know who the Antichrist is before the rapture?

The Antichrist cannot be revealed until we are gone. We may be able to make an educated guess. We may hear of a world leader rising in power and by the time we get to heaven we will probably know who he is, but once we're in heaven we probably won't care!

16. Will we be with our family in heaven?

I believe that will be strictly up to each individual. The Bible indicates in heaven there is no marriage or giving in marriage. I believe if you want to remain together you can. It gets complicated when someone has been married more than one time!

17. Does the Pope have a part in end time events?

Many have speculated that whoever is Pope at the time of the Tribulation will be the Antichrist. I do not believe this is the case. I believe he will have a political position and be a political leader. This Antichrist will be a Jew and will not sit over a particular denomination or group of people. The religion of the Tribulation will probably be what we refer to as the New Age. It will be a combination of major religions, including those from ancient Egypt and Bablyon. Revelation 7 talks about a whore who sits on seven mountains. The seven mountains represent the seven world empires that have controlled Israel through the centuries. The religions of all of those empires will be combined into one world religion.

18. How will the world explain the Rapture?

There will probably be lies told about our disappearance. The media may fabricate exotic tales. I believe just following the Rapture, masses of people will be looking for us and realize that what they had been told about the Rapture is true.

19. Will the Antichrist be a Jew?

The Antichrist will definitely be of Jewish lineage. He will probably come from the tribe of Dan. When Jacob prophesied over his twelve sons, it was prophesied a snake would come from the tribe of Dan. He talked of an adder that would come from a hidden position and would strike and kill. In reading the book of Revelation, it is interesting to note twelve tribes are mentioned, but the tribe of Dan is missing. However, there are still twelve tribes because the tribe of Joseph became two tribes—Ephraim and Manasseh—which make up for the tribe of Dan being removed.

20. Is 2000 years significant for the Church age?

There is no significance I know of. There are some very good teachings explaining that just as there were six days in creation and on the seventh day God rested, six-thousand years will pass and the Millennium will begin at the seven-hundreth year, because with the Lord one day is as a thousand years, but we still do not know the exact time of His coming.

21. Will the European Economic Community rise as a power before the rapture of the Church?

Yes, I believe very strongly the EEC will rise in power even though the Antichrist cannot be revealed until the

Church is removed. If Jesus doesn't return during the next few years, I believe we will see Europe become stronger and take a more signifcant role in world affairs.

22. How many nations will be involved in the Antichrist's one world government?

By the time Antichrist rises to power, there will be only ten and he will personally eliminate three of them.

23. When will the Old Testament saints be raptured?

Daniel 12:1-2 tells us the Old Testament saints will be resurrected at the Second Advent.

24. Are those left behind at the rapture the Bride of Christ?

No. Those saved during the Tribulation are not the Bride of Christ. They are friends of the bride and groom. The Church is the Bride of Christ. We will all eat together at the Marriage Supper of the Lamb.

25. How can people sin during the Millennium if there is a perfect environment?

People who become believers during the Tribulation and enter into the Millennium will have children during the Millennium. Those born during this time will either accept or reject Jesus as their Lord and Savior. Just as we are born again and still have the nature of the flesh because we have not received our resurrection bodies, the millennial saints will also have the nature of the flesh. Because of the nature of the flesh, even without the influence of Satan in the earth, an individual can reject Jesus. There are only two ways to be rid of the nature of the flesh: *die* or receive a *resurrection body.* People who are in heaven right now do not have the nature of the flesh because their physical bodies are dead. When they receive their resurrection body, it will not have the nature of the flesh. At the end of the Millennium, the millennial saints will receive their resurrection body.

26. Two-thirds of the angels did not follow Satan. Will they ever change their minds and choose to follow Satan instead of God?

No. God created the angels with wills but they were created differently than man. The Lord presented the angels with a one-time choice. He told them to choose whether they would follow Him or Satan. He let them know that their decision would be final and there would be not turning back.

27. Is the Holy Spirit hindering the revealing of Antichrist?

No. The Church is hindering Satan and his kingdom from being revealed. When the Church is raptured, the Holy Spirit will remain on earth. Signs, wonders, and miracles will take place during the Tribulation. The two witnesses will perform signs and wonders by the Holy Spirit.

28. Is it wrong to use a debit card; is it part of Satan's kingdom?

No. Anything created comes from the mind of God. Satan can only pervert what God has created. We should not fear technology. The Antichrist will pervert what God intended to bless His children with. The ability to speed up business transactions, telephone calls—all of the ways we are benefited by the technology of our day—is to bless us, save us time so that we have more time to invest in God's kingdom. Those who receive the mark of the beast will only choose that mark during the Tribulation and will not be saved. At one time television was considered the doorway into hell. One day Christians woke up and realized they could use this technology to spread the gospel. There may come a day when you have to swipe a card to give money into the offering. If technology advances to that point that is fine with me. I do not fear technology. Most any invention can be used to help spread the gospel.

A Prayer to Receive Jesus as Savior

Dear Heavenly Father,

*You said in Your Word, "If you confess with your mouth, 'Jesus is Lord,' and believe in your heart that God raised him from the dead, **you will be saved**" (Romans 10:9).*

I believe in my heart that Jesus Christ is the Son of God. I believe He died on the cross for my sins, and that He was raised from the dead. I now confess Jesus as my Lord, so I know, Father, that according to Your Word, I am now saved!

Thank You, Father, for forgiving me and for giving me the gift of the new birth. In Jesus' name.

Amen.

Meet Bob Yandian

Since 1980, Bob Yandian has been pastor of Grace Church, with a vibrant and growing congregation in his hometown of Tulsa, Oklahoma. He has a weekly teaching radio broadcast called *Precepts with Bob Yandian*. He is founder of *Grace School of Ministry*, a two-year ministerial training school.

Bob is widely acknowledged as one of the most knowledgeable Bible teachers of this generation. His practical insight and wisdom into the Word of God has helped countless people around the world live successfully in every arena of the daily Christian life.

In addition to the sale of over 200,000 books, CDs, and tapes world-wide, more than 22,000 books, CDs, and tapes have been donated to Bible schools, missionaries, prisoners, and people in need throughout the United States and around the world through *Bob Yandian Ministries.*

Bob attended *Southwestern College* and is also a graduate of *Trinity Bible College*. He has served as both instructor and Dean of Instructors at *Rhema Bible Training Center* in Broken Arrow, Oklahoma.